LOSING AND LIVING

David Maldwyn Owen was brought up in Haver-
fordwest, Dyfed. He is now a Minister in the
United Reformed Church in Reigate, Surrey and
also works part-time as a hospital chaplain. From
1981 to 1990 he wrote a religious column in
Woman's Weekly magazine which reached a read-
ership of several million. He writes regularly for
the International Bible Reading Association and
his previous book for Triangle was *Something of
a Saint: The lives and prayers of 52 famous
Christians*.

Dedicated to the Members and Friends
of Reigate Park Church
whom I have known over twenty-seven years,
and to those who have shared with me
in its pastoral work.

Losing and Living

THOUGHTS ON
EVERY KIND OF GRIEVING

Compiled and introduced by
DAVID M. OWEN

TRI△NGLE

First published 1991
Triangle
SPCK
Holy Trinity Church
Marylebone Road
London NW1 4DU

British Library Cataloguing in Publication Data

Owen, David M. (David Maldwyn), *1934*–
Losing and living : thoughts on every kind
of grieving.
I. Title
248.86

ISBN 1281045534

Typeset by Inforum Typesetting, Portsmouth
Printed in Great Britain by
BPCC Hazell Books
Aylesbury, Bucks
Member of BPCC Ltd

Contents

Preface

Life from birth to death consists of attachments and detachments, of gains and losses. Birth itself separates us from our mother's body; in the intervening years we form relationships with our parents, loved ones, friends and countless others whom we meet. We receive an education, qualify for a career, acquire possessions, and develop a personal character and religious faith. But just as commonly we experience detachments; we lose loved ones and friends, we change or lose jobs, we suffer ill-health and setbacks, part with material things, and in the end death brings about the irrevocable detachment of our earthly ties.

Job in the Old Testament struck a note of appreciation and realism: 'The Lord gives, and the Lord takes away; blessed be the name of the Lord' (Job 1.21 NEB). All too often our losses overwhelm us, we dwell on them so much and succumb to self-pity, we turn against God and forget to be grateful for all we have received and still possess, by which our lives are blessed.

There is 'a time to lose' said the writer of Ecclesiastes (3.6 NEB). Whatever he meant by 'lose', it goes against the grain, because we prefer success to failure. But he spoke a truism. There's an old saying, 'Losing renders sager.' Without loss we are never really put to the test. Just as a boat's rigging is never tested by fair-weather sailing, so strength of character is never tested without deprivations. Losing is as important as gaining, and just as positive.

Or did he have in mind those sins and faults that we all need to lose that spoil our characters? The author of Hebrews said, 'We must throw off every encumbrance, every sin to which we cling' (12.1 NEB). Only by casting out the bad can we make room for the good.

If by 'a time to lose' the author of Ecclesiastes meant that most painful of losses we suffer through the death of a dear one, at least he does us a service by reminding us of its inevitability, for we can easily take our closest relationships for granted and be unprepared for the sorrow of parting. Bereavement is unavoidable if we love someone, and we know this, yet it can take us unawares, leave us shattered, and linger a long time before we experience recovery.

It is as we turn to Jesus in the gospels, and to the teaching of the New Testament as a whole, that life's losses lose their bitter sting. The Christian faith puts them into perspective, converts them from negative to positive, and provides the strength and hope to continue living. Jesus cared about things that were lost. Chapter fifteen of Luke is the Gospel's Lost Property chapter – lost sheep, lost coin, a lost son – illustrative of our Lord's mission, and elsewhere the evangelist records Jesus' declaration: 'The Son of Man has come to seek and save what is lost' (Luke 19.10 NEB). It is to our great comfort that Jesus knew failure and suffered bereavement. He is the Christ of the cross, but also of the empty tomb. Through his teaching, example, death and resurrection he enables us to meet our losses and to go on living. This book, *Losing and Living*, makes that assertion; we can go on living after losing because God in Christ is with us in our tribulations, and holds before us the gift of eternal life.

Losing and Living is largely an anthology, drawing on the insights of the Bible and the wisdom of many writers. Two-thirds of the book relates to the loss of life and the experience of facing death and coping with bereavement. The remainder reflects on such losses as good health (due to advancing age or otherwise), faith, happiness and patience – ten in all, and doubtless others can be added.

My original manuscript was a great deal larger than the size of this book – indicative of the subject's boundless scope and the wealth of accumulative thought. I trust that what you read will serve the purpose for which it is designed in providing reflection, comfort, strength and hope. I might just add that the idea for the book and its scope arises largely out of my own experience of ministry in the church. In fact, not a single item has passed me by – such is the church's humanity! But such, too, is the faith we hold.

David Maldwyn Owen
Reigate, 1991

PART ONE

The Loss That We Face

Not a day passes but thousands of people die, from old age, disease, accident, in conflict or by suicide. Each life, each death, is individual, and leaves someone behind to mourn and miss. In each experience we need help and comfort.

Death Most Common

Birth is common to us all, and so is death. We are born to live, hopefully into old age and in happiness through the years, but then we must depart this life. Death is the great leveller, for monarchs and peasants, saints and sinners all die.

Nor during our lifetime here can any of us avoid meeting death in others or the personal and painful experience of bereavement. We lose loved ones and colleagues, and the media daily records the passing of public figures and a host of names unknown to us. Each week in my hospital chaplaincy work I visit the maternity ward and discover the joys of new life, but almost as frequently I am at the crematorium or cemetery laying to rest the body of one whose life has been completed. Life and death are inextricably linked, and this is not at all a morbid thought; on the contrary, it is exciting, for it means our living is an adventure and responsibility, and our death a commitment and fulfilment.

We rightly put as much thought and energy into living as fully as we can. Whilst we are not expected to go around every day thinking about death, it would be irresponsible of us to be so preoccupied with the here and now that we never think of death at all.

We do need to think about it in order to

prepare ourselves for it, and we should learn to speak of it with greater ease. It is a perfectly natural occurrence, just like birth, but whilst we were not conscious of life in the womb, and could do nothing to prepare for our release into the outside world, we can prepare for our own death. Perhaps the actual moment of our dying will be an unconscious one, or it might be the most conscious and exhilarating we have ever known. In the meantime we can prepare ourselves for this momentous occasion – in fact, the whole of life is preparation time – and we should never be so busy with worldly pursuits that it loses its place in our thinking.

We prepare for dying and death by honestly and constantly facing the truth about our mortality. It is said that the great warrior king, Philip of Macedonia, in the fourth century BC, appointed a courtier to whisper to him every day, 'Philip, remember thou too art mortal.' He was wise enough to know he needed to heed the warning, lest he should think himself a god.

We too are mortal, in common with every human being of every age, without exception. But how sad if our preparation was merely to see us through to the end and then oblivion! We believe otherwise, for that would be a terrible travesty and total discouragement, indeed, a mockery of our aspirations. Mortal we are in body, but immortal in soul. Add to that age-long belief, which is not specifically Christian, the teaching of the New Testament of Christ's resurrection and ours, and we can face the end of our earthly life and its beyond with confidence and joy.

The Bonds of Death

The bonds of death encompassed me
and destructive torrents overtook me,
the bonds of Sheol tightened about me,
the snares of death were set to catch me.
When in anguish of heart I cried to the LORD
and called for help to my God,
he heard me from his temple,
and my cry reached his ears.

PSALM 18.4-6 REB

Do not gloat over the death of anyone;
remember we all must die.

ECCLESIASTICUS 8.7 REB

Death Knocks

Death knocks, as we know, at the door of the
cottage and of the castle. He stalks up the front-
garden and the steep steps of the semi-detached
villa, and plies the ornamental knocker so imper-
iously that the panels of imitation stained glass
quiver in the thin front-door.

MAX BEERBOHM

Those Before and After Me

When I think of those who have preceded me, I
feel as if I were at a party in the dead hour which
has to be got through after the Guests of Honour
have left.

When I think of those who will come after –

5

or survive me, I feel as if I were taking part in the preparations for a feast, the joys of which I shall not share.

DAG HAMMARSKJÖLD

Involved in Mankind

Any man's death diminishes me, because I am involved in mankind; and therefore never send to know for whom the bell tolls; it tolls for thee.

JOHN DONNE

Death in Life

In the midst of life we are in death.

THE BOOK OF COMMON PRAYER

Death Does Matter

It is hard to have patience with people who say 'There is no death' or 'Death doesn't matter'. There is death. And whatever is matters. And whatever happens has consequences, and it and they are irrevocable and irreversible. You might as well say that birth doesn't matter. I look up at the night sky. Is anything more certain than that in all those vast times and spaces, if I were allowed to search them, I should nowhere find her face, her voice, her touch? She died. She is dead. Is the word so difficult to learn?

C.S. LEWIS

Treated All Alike

Death, the only immortal who treats us all alike, whose pity and whose peace and whose refuge are for all – the soiled and the pure, the rich and the poor, the loved and the unloved.

MARK TWAIN

But Life is Immortal

Men are indeed brothers, of each other and of the humblest form used by the one life. They should live as such; they should regard death from this point of view. Life never dies; only the forms of life. The opposite of death is not life, but birth. All that is born dies, but life is immortal . . .

CHRISTMAS HUMPHREYS

Death as Part of Life

Lord, it bothers me to hear so much talk about death. Death is a constant news item, and I keep hearing of the passing of people I have known. In my despondent moments, Lord, I'm inclined to think there's more death than life.

Forgive me for not seeing clearly that death is part of life, a rhythm as important as day and night, and that our comings and goings are in your hands, perfectly controlled and brought to fruition.

Help me to accept what is really your purpose for us all, and to meet all such happenings with a quiet faith.

DAVID M. OWEN

O Lord, Be with Us

O Lord, the first and the last,
  the beginning and the end:
you who were with us at our birth,
  be with us through our life;
you who are with us through our life,
  be with us at our death;
and because your mercy will not leave us then,
  grant that we die not,
    but rise to the life everlasting.

FROM *NEW EVERY MORNING*

Lord Have Mercy

When our powers are nearly done
At the going down of the sun
Kyrie eleison. Lord have mercy.

When we come to breath our last
When the gates of death are passed
Kyrie eleison. Lord have mercy.

DAVID ADAM

Simply for Love of You

Glorious God, give me grace to amend my life,
and to have an eye to my end without begrudg-
ing death, which to those who die in you, good
Lord, is the gate of a wealthy life.

Give me, good Lord, a longing to be with you,
not to avoid the calamities of this world, nor so
much to attain the joys of heaven, as simply for
love of you.

THOMAS MORE

To Live at Ease

Grant us wisdom, Lord, to live at ease in death's presence, not to fear it but to face it as your will for us.

VIRGINIA SLOYAN

Facing our Fears

Most of us have fears – fears of failure, loneliness, war, dangers facing our loved ones and, perhaps most of all, fears of the process of dying and of the 'Unknown Beyond'. How will we cope with pain and physical deterioration? Will we lose our mental faculties? Will death be oblivion cutting us off for ever from our cherished relationships? Or, if there is a judgement of us, how will we measure up? And if there is punishment for our sins, how will we bear it?

In his 'Hymn to God the Father' John Donne admits his fears about meeting death and of the consequences of his sins, but his hope rests in God's pardon and peace:

> I have a sin of fear that when I have spun
> My last thread, I shall perish on the shore;
> Swear by thy self that at my death, thy Sun
> Shall shine as it shines now, and heretofore;
> And having done that, thou hast done,
>   I have no more.

Fear in itself is not a sin. There are healthy fears that prevent recklessness and increase caution. A mountaineer or round-the-world yachtsman who had no fear of the elements would make a dangerous companion. Fear reminds us of life's vulnerability and fragility, and it is a healthy fear that produces fortitude and heroism. Our mistake is to let fear become fearfulness, so that we lose our composure and give way to despair. Such a condition is a denial of faith in God's providence.

I am sure God understands if we have fears in the face of dying and death, and does not condemn us for them. Let us confess them and seek reassurance from the Scriptures, through prayer and with the help of wise counsellors.

There is, though, a fear that must remain – the fear of God; not that of terror but of awe in the face of his mysteries that await us. When the Psalmist said, 'The fear of the Lord is the beginning of wisdom' (Psalm 111.10 NEB), he did not mean that we are to be frightened of him and so dread his presence, rather that we have an awed regard for his holiness and a proper concern for those sins which offend and cause him pain. It is an attitude of reverence before him and a call to righteous living.

It is to our comfort and encouragement that Jesus feared his coming death. Shortly after he had told his disciples not to let their hearts be troubled his own heart was in distress. He dreaded the cup of suffering leading to death, and prayed for its removal, and that brings him wonderfully close to us in any fears that we might have. His eventual acceptance of the cup lay in his deep trust in God his Father, to whom at the end he committed his spirit.

Trust, not Despair

The Lord is my light and my salvation;
 I will fear no one.
The Lord protects me from all danger;
 I will never be afraid . . .
Trust in the Lord. Have faith, do not despair.
 Trust in the Lord.

PSALM 27.1, 14 GNB

You have rescued me from death
 and my feet from stumbling,
to walk in the presence of God,
 in the light of life.

PSALM 56.13 REB

Do not be afraid. I am the first and the last, and I
am the living one; for I was dead and now I am
alive for evermore, and I hold the keys of Death
and Death's domain.

REVELATION 1.18 NEB

As Fear in the Dark

Men fear death, as children fear to go in the dark;
and as that natural fear in children is increased
with tales, so is the other.

FRANCIS BACON

To Know not What, or Where

Death in itself is nothing; but we fear
To be we know not what, we know not where.

JOHN DRYDEN

No Tomorrow

Death has but one terror, that it has no tomorrow.

ERIC HOFFER

Eternally Forgotten

In the depth of the anxiety of having to die is the anxiety of being eternally forgotten.

PAUL TILLICH

As the Close of Hope

We dread life's termination as the close, not of enjoyment, but of hope.

WILLIAM HAZLITT

I Shall Love Death as Well

It is the same life that shoots in joy through the dust of the earth in numberless blades of grass, and breaks into tumultuous waves of leaves and flowers. It is the same life that is rocked in the ocean-cradle of birth and of death, in ebb and flow. Because I love this life, I know I shall love death as well.

RABINDRANATH TAGORE

Jesus in the Garden

When we turn to the most perfect life of all, we do not find that it was lived without fear. Indeed, we find recorded by a doctor a symptom of fear which shows a depth of anguish rarely realised in the lives of men. 'His sweat became, as it were, great drops of blood falling down upon the ground.' This is a symptom of extreme anguish of mind which is rarely witnessed. The courage of Jesus is not that negative quality based on literal fearlessness. Surely it is true to say that the measure of his courage was the measure of his overcome fear. One would have been impossible without the other. And when the shadow of the cross loomed up so close to him that even he cried, 'If it be possible to let this cup pass,' he proceeded to take such an attitude to calamity that he wrung from the situation the courage only commensurate with the fear which that situation was capable of producing.

I believe that he can bring men to the point when they realise that there is no situation capable of defeating the human spirit; when the measure of the most terrible calamity the mind can imagine becomes the measure of courage which can be made out of the situation in order to overcome it.

LESLIE D. WEATHERHEAD

To Live and Die

Teach me to live, that I may dread
The grave as little as my bed;

Teach me to die, that so I may
Rise glorious at the aweful day.

THOMAS KEN

Death – my Fears

What do I *fear* about death?
(1) Being unable to cope with it when it comes.
(2) Being cut off "prematurely," before I am ready. I have a nasty feeling that I shall be yanked unceremoniously out of this life, with all sorts of loose ends and unfinished business.
(3) What is probably worse: a dreary, drawn-out process of dying, with the family visiting and everyone getting depressed; with me getting weaker, like an old banger running out of power going up a steep hill.
(4) Being unable to receive the Sacraments, or at least make a proper act of repentance and spiritual Communion.
(5) The distress of those I love, and my distress with and for them.
(6) Dying messily and painfully, over a steering-wheel or collapsed in a lavatory.
(7) On the other hand, having *too much time*, so that I might lose my nerve and give way to cowardice or whining (verbally or inwardly), sinking into self-pity, etc.
(8) Dying unconscious or in my sleep. On the other hand, having experienced acute physical pain, I do not relish that either.

So, however I look at it, I must reconcile myself to the fact that my death will not be arranged perfectly and I must be ready to "die well"

15

whatever the circumstances. In fact, I want to *resign* myself to whatever death I die; or, rather, to God in my dying.

GRAHAM SMITH

Fear Knocked

Fear knocked at the door.
Faith answered.
No one was there.

ANONYMOUS

Death be not Proud

Death, be not proud, though some have called
   thee
Mighty and dreadful, for thou are not so;
For those whom thou thinkst thou dost
   overthrow
Die not, poor Death, nor yet canst thou kill me.
From rest and sleep, which but thy pictures be,
Much pleasure – then, from thee much more
   must flow;
And soonest our best men with thee do go,
Rest of their bones and soul's delivery.
Thou'rt slave to fate, chance, kings, and
   desperate men,
And dost with poison, war, and sickness dwell;
And poppy or charms can make us sleep as well,
And better than thy stroke. Why swellst thou
   then?
One short sleep past, we wake eternally,
And death shall be no more. Death, thou shalt
   die.

JOHN DONNE

16

I Fear no Ill

In death's dark vale I fear no ill
    With thee, dear Lord, beside me;
Thy rod and staff my comfort still,
    Thy cross before to guide me.

HENRY W. BAKER

Lord, I'm Afraid

Lord, I am afraid of dying. I think I love you and
want to be with you but the thought of going from
this world into the unknown is terrifying. I begin
to wonder if you exist. O Lord, help me, give me
some reassurance that you will be with me unto
the end of the world and beyond it into the next.

MICHAEL HOLLINGS AND ETTA GULLICK

From Griefs and Fears

From all my griefs and fears, O Lord,
    Thy mercy sets me free,
Whilst in the confidence of prayer
    My heart takes hold on Thee.

In midst of dangers, fears, and death,
    Thy goodness I'll adore,
And praise Thee for Thy mercies past,
    And humbly hope for more.

My life, while Thou preserv'st my life,
    Thy sacrifice shall be;
And O may death, when death shall come,
    Unite my soul to Thee!

JOSEPH ADDISON

Into Thy Hands

O Lord, into Thy hands I commend my spirit, and the spirits of all those whom I love. Into Thy hands I commend the spirits of all those who are fearful, of death or life, of principalities or powers, of things present or of things that may never come. Into Thy hands I commend the spirits of all those who fear change, more than they fear Thee, who put the law above justice, and order above love.

ALAN PATON

Living for Dying

The Anglican Series 3 Litany bids us pray, 'From violence, murder, and *dying unprepared*, Good Lord, deliver us.'

To die, prepared or unprepared, implies a period of life, long or short, in which we accept or reject that responsibility. We therefore see this world as a training ground for our meeting with death and the new life that awaits us beyond death. Death itself is a test of life's fundamental questions about belief and behaviour. How truly do I believe in God? What does my life here add up to? How well have I lived, and what have I done to make this world a better place?

If we are to find satisfactory answers to such deep ponderings we need to wrestle throughout life with the mystery and challenge of death. The Swiss psychiatrist Carl Jung saw death as a goal towards which we strive, so that to shrink from it is unhealthy for us. He argued that as we get older death ought to occupy our minds much more, and that if we thought more of death we should make more of life.

We confidently assert that our life in this world, and the world itself, are God's most basic and precious gifts to us, which he expects us to use wisely and well. When the Psalmist said, 'The earth is the Lord's and all that is in it, the world and those who dwell therein' (Psalm 24.1 NEB), he was expressing a positive faith that all he saw belonged to the Lord. His view was world affirming and not world denying, and this is important in our understanding of life as a preparation for death and the future life. Here we live to die, not in any morbid or negative sense, not as those who despise this world, and not as some eager religious martyrs who have too readily thrown their life away. Death will come to each of us in time; meanwhile let us live each day to the full, knowing that each day and each deed are important to what we are now and to what we shall be.

Fullness of Life

By gaining his life a man will lose it; by losing his life for my sake, he will gain it.

MATTHEW 10.39 (NEB)

I have come that they may have life, and may have it in all its fullness.

JOHN 10.10 (NEB)

Direction of Life

The preservation of life should be only a secondary concern, and the direction of it our principal.

JOSEPH ADDISON

Dignity of thy Nature

Live unto the Dignity of thy Nature, and leave it not disputable at last, whether thou hast been a Man.

THOMAS BROWNE

If a Man Would Live Well

If a man would live well, let him fetch his last day to him, and make it always his company-keeper.

JOHN BUNYAN

Take Care

Take care of your life; and the Lord will take care of your death.

GEORGE WHITFIELD

Taught to Live and Die

Lord, what wilt thou teach me?
I will teach thee to die and I will teach thee to live . . .
What need have I, Lord, of being taught how to die bodily? Surely it teaches itself when it comes.
He who puts his teaching off till then, will find it too late.

HENRY SUSO

No Total Death

Death is the final stage of growth in this life. There is no total death.

ELIZABETH KÜBLER-ROSS

Life – a Dying

All of life is itself a dying. My existence today is built upon the death of my yesterday; and my today will perish so that my tomorrow may come.

NORMAN PITTINGER

As We Live, so We Die

Death is going home, yet people are afraid of what will come so they do not want to die. If we do, if there is no mystery, we will not be afraid. There is also the question of conscience – 'I could have done better.' Very often as we live, so we die. Death is nothing but a continuation of life, the completion of life. The surrendering of the human body. But the heart and the soul live for ever. They do not die. Every religion has got eternity – another life; this life is not the end; people who believe it is, fear death. If it was properly explained that death was nothing but going home to God, then there would be no fear.

MOTHER TERESA

So Be my Passing

A late lark twitters from the quiet skies;
And from the west,
Where the sun, his day's work ended,
Lingers as in content,
There falls on the old grey city
An influence luminous and serene,
A shining peace.

The smoke ascends
In a rosy and golden haze. The spires
Shine, and are changed. In the valley
Shadows rise. The lark sings on. The sun,
Closing his benediction,
Sinks, and the darkening air
Thrills with a sense of the triumphing night –
Night with her train of stars
And her great gift of sleep.

So be my passing!
My task accomplished and the long day done,
My wages taken, and in my heart
Some late lark singing,
Let me be gathered to the quiet west,
The sundown splendid and serene,
Death.

W. E. HENLEY

Part of a Larger Pattern

I have an absolute conviction, without any qualification whatsoever, that this life that we live in time and space for threescore years and ten is not the whole story; that it is only part of a larger story. Therefore, death cannot be for others, or for one's self, an end, any more than birth is a beginning. Death is part of a larger pattern; it fits into a larger, eternal scale, not simply a time scale . . . I think of my own death as something which will transform my way of living into another mode of living rather than as an end; and one thinks of others whom one has loved and who have died as equally participating in that other existence, in that larger dimension. To me this is completely satisfying. I don't want to know any more than this.

MALCOLM MUGGERIDGE

Tuning Here

Since I am coming to that holy room
    Where with the choir of saints for evermore,
I shall be made thy music; as I come
    I tune the instrument here at the door
And what I must do then, think here before.

JOHN DONNE

For Life and Death are One

You would know the secret of death,
But how shall you find it unless you seek it in the
    heart of life?
The Owl, whose night-bound eyes are blind
    unto the day, cannot unveil the mystery of
    light,

If you would indeed behold the spirit of death,
  open your heart wide into the body of life,
For life and death are one, even as the river and
  the sea are one.

KAHLIL GIBRAN

The Lesson from Nature

In nature death is not the end of life, but a means
by which life is fulfilled and enriched; it has a
positive as well as a negative element. Those who
view death as the 'endless endingness of everything, all that going down into the grave' have, as
yet, failed to see that this gloom is dispelled by
the joy of endless beginnings, by all that life
emerging from the bud, the shell and the womb.

The decay of autumn is necessary for the coming of spring, the leaf falls that the bud may
grow, shell and womb that have sheltered the
growing life perish, but the life goes on to fulfil
its destiny. The widow mourning her husband
finds comfort in seeing his life and hers continu-
ing in their children and grandchildren.

JOHN COLE

Death a Fulfilment

Do not seek Death. Death will find you.
But seek the road which makes death a
fulfilment.

DAG HAMMARSKJÖLD

To Live Every Day

Who can tell what a day may bring forth? Cause
me therefore, gracious God, to live every day as

if it were to be my last, for I know not but that it may be such. Cause me to live now as I shall wish I had done when I come to die. O grant that I may not die with any guilt on my conscience, or any known sin unrepented of, but that I may be found in Christ, who is my only Saviour and Redeemer.

THOMAS À KEMPIS

Thanks for Life

I thank Thee, God, that I have lived
In this great world and known its many joys;
The song of birds, the strong, sweet scent of hay
And cooling breezes in the secret dusk,
The flaming sunsets at the close of day,
Hills, and the lonely, heather-covered moors,
Music at night, and moonlight on the sea,
The beat of waves upon the rocky shore
And wild, white spray, flung high in ecstasy:
The faithful eyes of dogs, and treasured books.
The love of kin and fellowship of friends,
And all that makes life dear and beautiful.
I thank Thee, too, that there has come to me
A little sorrow and, sometimes, defeat,
A little heartache and the loneliness
That comes with parting, and the word,
    'Goodbye',
Dawn breaking after dreary hours of pain,
When I discovered that night's gloom must yield
And morning light break through to me again.
Because of these and other blessings poured
Unasked upon my wondering head,
Because I know that there is yet to come

An even richer and more glorious life,
And most of all, because Thine only Son
Once sacrificed life's loveliness for me –
I thank Thee, God, that I have lived.

ELIZABETH, COUNTESS OF CRAVEN

Lord, You are Life

Jesus, Lord, you are life
Always and everywhere;
In creation you are life,
In the world you are life,
In the Church you are life.
When death shall still our mortal bodies,
You, Lord, will be our life eternally.

DAVID M. OWEN

Work and Life

God give me work
Till my life shall end,
And life
Till my work is done.

CHARLES F. SHEPHERD

And our Work is Done

O Lord, support us all the day long of this troublous life, until the shadows lengthen, and the evening comes, and the busy world is hushed, the fever of life is over, and our work is done. Then, Lord, in your mercy, grant us safe lodging, a holy rest, and peace at the last; through Jesus Christ our Lord.

JOHN HENRY NEWMAN

Untimely, Unfulfilled

At Capernaum Jesus met with the sad experience of a child's terminal illness and parental distress. Jairus' cry said it all: 'My little daughter is at death's door, I beg you to come and lay your hands on her to cure her and save her life' (Mark 5.21–3, 35–43).

And at Nain, a young man, but still a mother's child had died, leaving her grief-stricken. The story is told in Luke 7.11–15, and it reveals a double tragedy. The woman had already suffered the loss of her husband, but with an only son as breadwinner she would have coped. Now she faced severe hardship. Luke's account of the funeral occasion reveals the deep compassion of Jesus, for when he saw the widow his heart went out to her. The meaning here is to be moved to the depths of one's being, and it was an emotion Jesus showed in other situations.

It is a heart-rending experience for any parent to lose a child, and indeed, for anyone else associated with the tragedy. I recall the funeral service I conducted of a sixteen-year-old girl killed in a car crash. The grief of her parents and school friends made it an occasion of intense pathos, and one of the most difficult services I've had to take.

A life cut short in infancy, childhood or

youth, seems a pointless waste, and evokes the most soul-searching questions. Children are meant to enjoy years of happiness, but why are some denied them? If God has a plan for each new life, why is it disrupted before reaching at least a measure of maturity?

We gain nothing and lose much by blaming God. Premature death is not his will. Jesus' love for children (Matthew 19.13–15) and high estimate of their value (Matthew 18.1–7) tell the true story – the kingdom of heaven is theirs, and they are a shining example of humility to all.

Why children die, why someone's life is terminated in the middle years when others go on to old age, will always seem unfair. And any talk about the quality of life being more important than the quantity of years, though deeply true, is not guaranteed to bring immediate comfort to distraught parents, to a young widow bereft of her equally young husband, or to her children dispossessed of their father.

Nor, indeed, does everyone at the time of intense grief find reassurance in talk of a future life in which the imbalance is redressed. (Close company and respectful silence will probably be of more help.) But such reasoning is not unsound, for if God is a loving Father, as Jesus asserted, then should we not trust him to provide amply for those whom we have loved and lost too soon? Many have found comfort in the thought that our departed children are safe in the love of Jesus, and are led by him to their fulfilment. So too the others who died in the middle life with so much left undone.

Alive in Jesus

To this day we believe Jesus showed that same deep concern for both sick and dying children and their sorrowing parents as he did at Nain.

The sorrow of this occasion in Nain was turned to joy, for this was one of Jesus' miracles when he raised the dead to life. In Luke 7.15 we find a lovely touch of tenderness, for as the dead man sat up and spoke we read, 'Jesus gave him back to his mother.'

Whilst that miracle does not become literally true, for parents and children are physically separated at death, it is true in a spiritual sense and in terms of our faith. The child whose body has been destroyed by disease and death is now alive and secure in Jesus, who is the resurrection and the life. It is this belief and hope that is entrusted to sorrowing parents – a child secure in the love of Christ, with whom one day there will be a reunion.

DAVID M. OWEN

The Bonding

The birth of a baby; the bonding of mother and infant; the fun and worries of childhood and teenage years; the friendship of mother and nearly-adult son – to be followed by sudden and total separation: will I ever be whole again after all that?

Chinks of light are appearing at the end of the tunnel. God is answering prayer in his own time and way.

ELIZABETH BOOT

Further Stages of Growth

For those who die young or tragically death is far from being a friend . . . it raises also the question of the possibility of further stages of growth after this life. So many die with lives cut short. Too many die after a lifetime of frustration and lack of fulfilment. If death is to be a friend of all there must be not only the possibility of life beyond it but a life in which all that has been stunted or nipped in the bud is enabled to grow.

RICHARD HARRIES

Fulfilment Waits

When I reflect with what relentless speed
Our life moves onward to its earthly goal,
While every passing season takes its toll
Of tasks unfinished, hopes that miss their meed;

Then answers Faith, rebuking my despair,
'Fulfilment waits thee past the gates of death;
Else were thy little life a transient breath;
God made thee not as spume to waste in air.'

For every rapturous reaching for the stars,
Each dream that fades, each thirst unsatisfied,
Is earnest of a joy no shadow mars,
Brief foretaste here of splendours that abide,
A home of bliss past man's imagining,
Lit by the fadeless beauty of the King.

JACK WINSLOW

The Unfinisheds

We cannot judge a biography by its length, by the number of pages in it; we must judge by the richness of the contents . . . Sometimes the 'unfinisheds' are among the most beautiful symphonies.

VICTOR FRANKL

For One Born Dead

What ceremony can we fit
You into now? If you had come
Out of a warm and noisy room
To this, there'd be an opposite
For us to know you by. We could
Imagine you in lively mood

And then look at the other side,
The mood drawn out of you, the breath
Defeated by the power of death.
But we have never seen you stride
Ambitiously the world we know.
You could not come and yet you go.

But there is nothing now to mar
Your clear refusal of our world.
Not in our memories can we mould
You or distort your character.
Then all our consolation is
That grief can be as pure as this.

ELIZABETH JENNINGS

What Greater Pain?

What greater pain could mortals have than this: to see their children dead before their eyes?

EURIPIDES

Without having Lived

To die is poignantly bitter, but the idea of having to die without having lived is unbearable.

ERICH FROMM

The Child We have Lost

Loving Father, the child we have lost in death was part of us, flesh of our flesh, and we feel bereft and incomplete, like losing a limb that can never be restored.

Help us to trust you for your promise of new life and new beginnings. Reassure us that the words Jesus spoke so long ago, he speaks still: 'Let the children come to me, for the kingdom of heaven is theirs.' And while we wait to meet again in the life after death, help us to live lovingly and happily with the rest of our family.

We pray through him who, from the cross, saw his mother's grief, Jesus Christ our living Lord.

DAVID M. OWEN

Sorrowing Hearts

O God, our heavenly Father, whose ways are hidden and thy works wonderful, comfort, we pray thee, this woman and her husband whose hearts are heavy with sorrow. Surround them with thy protection, and grant them grace to face the future with good courage and hope. Teach them to use this pain in deeper sympathy for all who suffer, so that they may share in thy work of turning sorrow into joy; through Jesus Christ our Lord.

GUILD OF HEALTH

Lord, I am Dying Now

Lord, I am dying now. There is so much I wanted to do, so much I never did. I look back on life and think if only. . . . But now, Lord, I'm tired. I can't think properly. Let me give everything over to you, sort it out for me, dear Lord, that I may rest in peace.

MICHAEL HOLLINGS AND ETTA GULLICK

Be Near Me, Lord

Be near when I am dying,
    O show Thy cross to me!
And for my succour flying,
    Come, Lord, to set me free.
These eyes, new faith receiving,
    From Jesus shall not move,
For he who dies believing,
    Dies safely through Thy love.

PAULUS GERHARDT

The Tragic Choice

Tom had been married to Eileen for five years – I had conducted their wedding service – but work and personal problems proved too much for him, and he committed suicide by drowning. I then had the sad task of taking his funeral service, and I recall the terrible grief of his wife and other members of the family, and their particular feelings of hurt and guilt which usually accompany loss through suicide.

Anyone who has suffered this kind of bereavement will know the need for loving support. Thankfully, Christian opinion has moved from cruel condemnation of someone who has taken his own life to one of compassion. We may have difficulty in condoning the act, but are comforted by the approach that reaches out in understanding and acceptance of the distress that has driven a person to such an extremity, for this is a sickness and not a sin.

People who threaten to take their own lives must be taken seriously. Their threat is a distress signal – a cry for help, and they need skilled counselling and care. Suicidal distress may be caused by chronic illness in which a person suffers intense pain. Someone who has been diagnosed as terminally ill may wish to avoid prolonged suffering or being a burden on others.

Victims of loss also contemplate suicide – the loss of a loved one through death or divorce, or the loss of a job with its accompanying stigma and insecurity. And invariably there is depression, characterised by feelings of worthlessness, hopelessness, guilt, loss of appetite and sexual desire, loss of weight, chronic insomnia, apathy and fatigue. The depressed person often withdraws from society and loses interest even in once-prized activities.

Not all the skilled help offered and accepted by a suicidal person removes the need for ordinary compassion – indeed, it supplements it. An hour spent in company with a friend over a cup of tea, an invitation to a meal, to a car ride in the countryside – just warm, caring friendship – can often work wonders. To love in that kind of way is to walk very close to God.

Despair

I would prefer death to all my sufferings. I am in despair, I would not go on living; leave me alone, for my life is but a vapour.

JOB 7.15–16 NEB

Come to me, all who labour and are heavy-laden, and I will give you rest. Take my yoke upon you . . . and you will find rest for your souls.

MATTHEW 11.28–9 RSV

Expression of Distress

In general, the suicidal person is in a disorganized, chaotic state. He feels helpless, hopeless and is looking desperately for assistance. He is usually anxious, confused, and frequently hostile. He feels lonely, alone, and rejected, and thinks that no one loves him. His suicidal behaviour can best be understood as an expression of his severe emotional distress.

SUICIDE PREVENTION CENTRE

Tribulation

The New Testament scholar William Barclay reminds us that the meaning of the Greek word translated 'tribulation' means 'pressure', and that in classical Greek it is used, for instance, of a man tortured to death by being slowly crushed by a great boulder laid on him. He writes: 'There is the pressure of work, the pressure of worry, the pressure of material circumstances, the pressure of opposition and antagonism and persecution. Under that pressure many people collapse. Life becomes too much for them; physically and mentally they cannot bear the strain.'

I believe that those who in this life find the strain too much are met in death by the mercy of God. We take comfort in that, and trust that those who lost their peace here are at peace in him, who alone understands the agonies that beset us in this mortal life.

DAVID M. OWEN

Up Against It

Most individual creatures, since life began, have been up against it. . . . They have had to respond to the unresting antagonism of their circumstances.

H.G. WELLS

To Look at your Life Again

I had thought that your death
Was a waste and a destruction,
A pain of grief hardly to be endured.
I am only beginning to learn
That your life was a gift and a growing
And a loving left with me.
The desperation of death
Destroyed the existence of love.
But the fact of death
Cannot destroy what has been given.
I am learning to look at your life again
Instead of your death and your departing.

MARJORIE PIZER

But She Could Not Pull Out of It

We had all felt and seen it coming, Lord. She was so deeply sad, depressed beyond all human endurance. The doctors tried drugs and her friends laughter and firmness, patience and love. But she could not pull out of it. And so she took that overdose and died. Well, Lord, I feel in my heart that you could have boundless love and care and compassion for her and that now she will never more be depressed, but know the fullness of joy and peace in you. So thus I pray in confidence, Lord.

MICHAEL HOLLINGS AND ETTA GULLICK

You Alone Know what he Suffered

Lord, we cannot understand why he took his own life. You alone know what he suffered. Forgive our lack of understanding, and give him the comfort and compassion which we so unthinkingly failed to give. Lord, we pray that he may rest in peace with you in the warmth of your love; and, Lord, give support to his family and those close to him through your healing and redeeming love which you showed us in your Son.

MICHAEL HOLLINGS AND ETTA GULLICK

Come Unto Me

We remember in the presence of God
Our neighbours who find no purpose in life and
    no joy in living.
Jesus said
    Come unto me.
In the name of Jesus the crucified
We try to imagine the mood of despair
And the hatred of one's own body
Which makes men long for death.
Jesus said
    Come unto me.
Many of us have known such moods from time
    to time.

Perhaps some of us have been near to suicide
   itself.
Let us be honest with ourselves and with God.
And in our heart of hearts admit to him what we
   painfully try to forget.
Jesus said
   Come unto me.
With ourselves let us include in loving prayer
Those we may never meet and do not know
Who hate what they have done or what they are
And who cannot face life any more;
Many in our community, our own street, in our
   own church.
Jesus said
   Come unto me.
Lord God, with us or without us,
By your word or by your deed,
Save, and redeem and give them your new life
today. Amen.

SIMON H. BAYNES

Christ My Helper

You, O Christ, have been there before me.

The darker the torment that drags me down,
   the brighter and higher I rise with you.
The sorer the grief that tears me apart,
   the sweeter the healing and joy you bring.
The stronger the death that locks me fast,
   the surer your Life that sets me free.

PRAYER FELLOWSHIP HANDBOOK

40

When Disaster Strikes

When a coal tip hurtled down on to a school at Aberfan in 1966, killing 116 children, one man was heard to retort, 'Where was God when this lot came down?' Behind the question lay either a denial of God's existence, or an assertion that if there was a God, he was unable to control what had happened, or was unaware of it or indifferent to it.

Loss of life or injury as a result of such disasters constitutes the atheist's best weapon of attack against belief in God. How can a God of love in control of his world allow this to happen? Following most tragedies it is our tendency to blame someone. In the case of disease leading to death, or of earthquake, hurricane, flood or drought, who is to blame but God?

People in Old Testament times clearly saw God as the sole Creator of the world, and initiator of all that happens. See, for example, Isaiah 4.5, 7: 'I make the light, I create darkness, author alike of prosperity and trouble. I, the Lord, do all these things' (NEB). They mostly believed too that human disasters were sent by God as punishment for sin, and that he rewarded the righteous with prosperity. The value of the Book of Job lies in its challenge at least to the easy notion of divine punishment, for Job had lived an upright life, yet had suffered appallingly.

In a true sense, all sin brings suffering of a kind. There is the suffering caused by drunken drivers or negligent engineers. In the case of Aberfan there had been prior warnings of the dangerous coal tip. We cannot flout basic physical or moral laws without consequences. Much suffering is caused by sin, but not all. We have all known saintly people upon whom great personal disaster has fallen – a reminder that sun and rain fall indiscriminately on the just and unjust, on good and bad alike. The righteous have no more immunity against disaster than the unrighteous.

In the New Testament we find Jesus unwilling to accept the traditional glib answers. With reference to the falling tower of Siloam and loss of life (Luke 13.1–5), he repudiates the belief that this disaster was God's punishment for people's sins. According to the interpretation of one scholar, Jesus is saying in effect, 'We don't know why the Galileans and the eighteen workmen of Siloam died. They were neither better nor worse than their fellows. The real question for us is not why they were taken, but why are we left?'

Jesus' disciples, too, in line with Old Testament thinking, posed the same dilemma when confronted with the man born blind: 'Who sinned, this man or his parents, that he was born blind?' (John 9.2). Jesus refused to relate his blindness to either of the parents, adding, 'He was born blind so that God's power might be displayed in curing him.' We must not take this to mean that he had suffered his blindness all those years in order that Jesus might perform a miracle of healing that would delight the crowd. Rather, he says, don't question as to why this man was born blind or who is to blame, ask instead, what God is going to do in this situation – the implication being that God wishes to act compassionately on the man's behalf.

Of course we will debate the moral and spiritual implications of tragedies, whether natural or man-made. Human negligence that has brought about someone's death is more clearly defined and dealt with, whereas natural disasters, so called 'acts of God', can often cause tremors in our faith. But we can be sure of this. It is quite contrary to our Christian belief in a loving Father to say that he releases natural elements like storm or earthquake to hurt or correct us, or that he is unconcerned about us when we are caught up in a disaster. His created world is made up of sunshine, rain and wind, of ocean and landscape, all of which contain elements that are dangerous to us humans, and that require our utmost caution. To provide absolute protection would mean removing us from planet earth altogether, or else greatly limiting our freedom of movement and choice.

To ask why God allows suffering is quite in order, and even goes some way to answering the problem. We may not say God sends or causes suffering, for this would be to involve him in an absurd contradiction, since our knowledge of him is clearly that he wills the relief of suffering. We are sure that he has granted freedom to his created order in which disasters and sorrows occur, as what H. H. Farmer suggested in his phrase 'the relative independence of the world', meaning that God does not interrupt the process of creation he has set in motion. He has given integrity to nature, and it is within this 'relative independence' that disasters, diseases and accidents occur. We know that God does not want any of us to suffer, for he is on the side of health and happiness.

Let us realise that creation is continuous. God is still at work in evolving his world. The process he began millions of years ago in shaping the earth's crust he continues, even though human beings are on the scene, and are sometimes affected by upheavals in the process. Teilhard de Chardin said, 'In all evolution we have to reckon with failures and mistakes.'

Truly this is life, and we have to accept it. What happens to us here, whether we live for many years or a few, whether in sickness or in health, is an inexplicable fact of creation. Whilst suffering and death will be lessened by taking extra precautions, and indeed, by sinning less, they can never be totally avoided. Of course we might suffer less deprivation if we avoid falling in love and getting married and having children, or making friendships or assuming responsibilities, but would we really want this? We who are artists in living must endure the agony if we are to enjoy the ecstasy.

However intense our questioning, we are left with the ever recurring fact of human tragedies. To blame God is pointless and unnecessary: better to offer him the service of our skills and the generous gifts of our money to help where we can, and to be part of his concern to take action. 'Although the world is full of suffering,' wrote Helen Keller, who was blind, deaf and dumb, 'it is also full of the overcoming of it.'

The religion of Jesus calls us to move beyond speculation. It bids us see him exercising deeds of love toward the needy, and in the cross his own supreme involvement in our human scene, facing the worst that could happen, yet turning history's blackest day into one of brightness and joy.

In Spite of all

Though the fig tree do not blossom,
    nor fruit be on the vines,
the produce of the olive fail
    and the fields yield no food,
the flock be cut off from the fold
    and there be no herd in the stalls,
yet I will rejoice in the Lord,
I will joy in the God of my salvation.

HABAKKUK 3.17–18 RSV

What Sort of World?

We may not say that God 'creates' moral evil, though we have to admit that he permits it and to that extent has some responsibility for it. But what would we have? It is conceivable that God might have created the entire world a garden of Eden, a ready-made and perfect welfare state,

45

with no crafty serpent and no ravening carnivores to spoil it. Such a world would not be a better world than the world we know. Instead of being moral agents, capable of doing right and wrong, we should have been automata. Better than that, the world as it is, for all its guilt and shame. The world which God created is a world in which there is the constant tension of opposites, light and darkness, weal and woe, good and evil.

C.R. NORTH

Correctly Relating

Relating a clubfoot to God may be the ruin of a man's religion. Relating God to a clubfoot may be the making of a man's life.

PAUL SCHERER

No Intervention

'Why doesn't God *stop* evil and cruel men from causing so much suffering?' This is a very natural and understandable question, but how exactly could such intervention be arranged without interfering with the gift of personal choice? Are we to imagine the possessor of a cruel tongue to be struck dumb, the writer of irresponsible and harmful newspaper articles visited with writer's cramp, or the cruel and vindictive husband to find himself completely paralysed? Even if we limit God's intervention to the reinforcement of the voice of conscience, what can be done where conscience is disregarded or has been silenced through persistent suppression? The moment we begin to envisage such interventions, the whole structure of human free will is destroyed.

J.B. PHILLIPS

Pattern and Illumination

I think it is part of the pattern of life. What's more I think it's an essential part. Imagine human life being drained of suffering! If you could find some means of doing that, you would not ennoble it; you would demean it. Everything I have learnt, whatever it might be – very little I fear – has been learnt through suffering.

MALCOLM MUGGERIDGE

To God We Cried

The storm upon us fell,
The floods around us rose;
The depths of death and hell
Seemed on our souls to close;
To God we cried in strong despair,
He heard, and came to help our prayer.

HENRY FRANCIS LYTE

God in the Midst

Ernest Gordon has written of his experience in a Burma death-camp. There in the squalor and starvation, where demoralized prisoners were dying like flies, a little group of men – none of them churchmen or believers, not even Gordon himself – began to read the New Testament.

47

Gordon writes: 'In the light of our new under-standing, the Crucifixion was seen as being of the utmost relevance to our situation. A God who remained indifferent to the plight of his creatures was not a God with whom we could agree. The Crucifixion, however, told us that God was in our midst, suffering with us. . . . We could see that God was not indifferent to such suffering. We stopped complaining about our own. Faith could not save us from it, but it would take us through it. We looked at the Cross and took strength from the knowledge that it gave us, that God was in our midst.'

Gordon can't explain why men have to suffer as they do. Nor could George Matheson. Nor can I. But we know the place where we can learn what matters more – how to meet it and how it can be used. And we offer to you the Person through whose pain we find the way to God, for it was God's way to us. 'Christ also hath once suffered for sins, the just for the unjust, that he might bring us to God.'

DAVID H.C. READ

Why, Lord?

O Creator of the universe, when earthquakes, cyclones,
floods and droughts strike we ask why?
Why, if you are loving as well as all-powerful,
did you create a world in which these disasters happen
and innocent people suffer so helplessly?

To that question we can give no answer.
Faith says, God knows.
He made the world and pronounced it good
and in Christ he suffers with us.

We praise you, suffering Father of Jesus,
for your grace shown in those whose faith
    remains firm
when disasters destroy all their possessions
and even their loved ones;

For your grace shown in those whose love
    remains sure,
who are concerned with others, who put
    themselves last;
for your grace in those who offer help,
who leave comfort and work long hours in tough
    conditions
to relieve suffering, we praise you.

PRAYER FELLOWSHIP HANDBOOK

Suffering Disturbs Me

Lord, suffering disturbs me, oppresses me.
I don't understand why you allow it.
Why, Lord?

Why this innocent child who has been moaning
    for a week, horribly burned?
This man who has been dying for three days and
    three nights, calling for his mother?
This woman with cancer who in one month
    seems ten years older?

49

This worker fallen from his scaffolding, a broken
   puppet less than twenty years old?
This stranger, poor isolated wreck, who is one
   great open sore?
This woman in a cast, lying on a board for more
   than thirty years?
Why, Lord?
I don't understand.
Why this suffering in the World that shocks,
   isolates, revolts, shatters?
Why this hideous suffering that strikes blindly
   without seeming cause,
Falling unjustly on the good, and sparing the
   evil,
Which seems to withdraw, conquered by
   science, but comes back in another form, more
   powerful and more subtle?
I don't understand.
Suffering is odious and frightens me.
Why these people, Lord, and not others?
Why these, and not me?

Son, it is not I, your God, who has willed
   suffering, it is men.
They have brought it into the world in bringing
   sin,
Because sin is disorder, and disorder hurts.
There is for every sin, somewhere in the world
   and in time, a corresponding suffering.
And the more sins there are, the more suffering.

But I came, and I took all your sufferings upon
   me, as I took all your sins,
I took them and suffered them before you.

50

I transformed them, I made of them a treasure.
They are still an evil, but an evil with a purpose,
For through your sufferings, I accomplish
   redemption.

MICHEL QUOIST

For Those in Trouble

Almighty and ever loving God, the comfort of
the sad, the strength of the suffering: let the
prayers of all who cry out of any tribulation
come unto you; and to every soul that is distressed grant mercy, refreshment and peace; for
the sake of Jesus Christ our Lord. Amen.

MARGARET GIRDLESTONE

They Died in War

Early in the Second World War my uncle, who was a pilot officer, and his crew, were shot down over Germany. I was only eight years old at the time but I still remember the grief-stricken faces of my grandparents when they received the news that their son was 'missing, believed killed'. For some time they clung to the faint hope that he had not lost his life, and was a prisoner of war, but their worst fears were then confirmed. It was a shattering blow that they never really got over.

They were just parents among thousands of others to suffer such a stunning loss. Near to where I lived as a boy were two young brothers. Both lost their lives in the war when their ship was torpedoed, leaving their parents doubly devastated. A woman described to me the loss of her son in war as 'worse than losing a limb'. A nation at war is a nation of countless broken hearts and ruined lives.

People who lose a loved one in war often agonise over its worthwhileness or otherwise. To lose someone in a 'just war' for reasons of self-defence brings some reassurance at least to the bereaved, whereas to lose in a war they deem futile, carries a more bitter sting. During a two months' stay in the United States eight years after the Vietnam War, I met with a great deal of resentment at America's involvement in it, which had resulted in an appalling loss of life.

Among the sorrows of war is the inability of grieving relatives to bury their dead. Some are interred in war graves, later to be visited, but as many again perish without trace. My uncle's body was never found; the most that could be granted was his name inscribed among thousands of his Air Force compatriots at the Runnymead memorial, and also at the war memorial in his home town.

Public cenotaphs are of great importance. It is true, most of us pass them by without a thought except for the annual occasion of Remembrance Sunday, too busy to recall their significance; but they bear a timeless recollection of our conflicts, 'lest we forget', and symbolise our longing for peace 'when war shall be no more'.

They are reminders in stone of the tragic loss of life during this twentieth century. In the 1914–18 war, 'the war to end all wars', eight and a half million members of the Forces of all nations are said to have perished, and twenty-one million wounded. The Second World War was even more devastating, with twenty-two million military and civilian dead and thirty-four million wounded. It was the war in which the Nazis exterminated six million Jews – a crime that has defiled the world. Anyone who visits Yad Vashem in Jerusalem, the Memorial to the Holocaust, will have its horrors painfully brought home. I stood one day in its Hall of Remembrance, before the Eternal Flame and the names of the twenty-one death camps. Beside me stood a woman, frail and weeping. As I put an arm around her she told me in her anguish, simply, 'I was at Auschwitz.' As she went away and mingled again with the crowd, what brutality I wondered had she seen, what fear, what awful death, what personal loss? My eyes filled with tears as she brought home to me in that unforgettable moment the bitter pangs of war.

Since those terrible years there has been conflict in Korea, Vietnam, Afghanistan, the Falklands, the Middle East, and skirmishes in many places. We have seen pictures of brutalities and death in South Africa, and much of that continent is torn with discord. The political and religious divide in Northern Ireland constantly throws up its bitter loss of life, of soldiers, police officers and civilians.

Let our memorials in stone, our plaques in public places, our Remembrance Day services go on reminding us of the sorrows of war, however necessary, and the cost of our conflicts in terms of human life. Let them be symbols of our resolve, for to remember the dead without striving to act as peacemakers in our relationships is to dishonour them. Let our memorials tell of courage and sacrifice, and of a tomorrow better than yesterday; let them depict the cross of Christ, with all its shame, and in all its glory.

World in Ruin

Just a little scrap of paper
In a yellow envelope,
And the whole world is in ruin,
    Even hope.

G.A. STUDDERT KENNEDY

Where the World Ended

In Pilsen,
Twenty-six Station Road,
she climbed to the Third Floor
up stairs which were all that was left
of the whole house,
she opened her door
full on to the sky,
stood gaping over the edge.

For this was the place
the world ended.

Then
she locked up carefully
lest someone steal
Sirius
or Aldebaran
from her kitchen,
went back downstairs
and settled herself
to wait
for the house to rise again
and for her husband to rise from the ashes
and for her children's hands and feet to be stuck
    back in place.

In the morning they found her
still as stone,
sparrows pecking her hands.

MIROSLAV HOLUB

In Time of War

They served their King and Country with all their strength and gave their lives to save their friends. 'Whosoever leads such a life need not care upon how short a warning it be taken from him.'

Courage and fortitude are lovely words,
And lovely are the virtues they define,
Yours was the courage, laughing soldier,
May the fortitude be mine.

SOURCE UNKNOWN

They Died for Us

We want to live. We did not ask to be born into a world of guns and bombs. We do not want to fight. Leave us alone, you statesmen and rulers, let us live our lives in peace. We want to live.

So did they, the boys, girls, men and women who lived, suffered and died in the wars. Of course they wanted to go on living; and yet, for some strange, inscrutable reason that God alone knows, they were destined for wounds and slaughter. God let them be killed. Before they died, many of them had to endure hell on earth. Somehow they struggled on. Where did they find the strength? Some, in the people they loved, or the country they loved, or the sheer animal will to survive; some, in their faith in God.

There were those who believed that they were giving themselves to build a world for us. They died for the future, for an ideal world that we could live in, an earth at peace. Now it is our turn to strive for peace on earth. War is not only made by statesmen. It is made by us, ordinary people who strive to achieve our own selfish ends, quarrelling and hating as we pursue our petty, sordid, self-seeking quest. We *can* make peace, with God's help, if we have faith, and hope, and love for one another. *We* are responsible for peace. Let us begin here, to build what the dead of the wars left unfinished. Perhaps we were not worth dying for: but without their sacrifice we would not be alive today.

Let us thank God for them, and let us honour them, in silence.

MICHAEL DAVIS

We Will Remember Them

They shall grow not old, as we that are left grow old:
Age shall not weary them, nor the years condemn.
At the going down of the sun and in the morning
We will remember them.

LAURENCE BINYON

Yet We are Friends

Hans Friedman was a German student at the University of Glasgow. He spent most of his childhood listening for the drone of British and American bombers approaching with their loads of destruction. He saw his home destroyed, his mother and father killed by Allied bombs. Hans detested the enemy. He stood before an audience composed of young British men who also knew something of air raids, buzz bombs, deaths of friends, relatives, and loved ones. 'There are many things that separate us,' Hans admitted, 'language, custom, tradition, history. I should hate you and you should hate me; yet we are friends because we have a common friend . . . Jesus Christ. I know of no other explanation.'

R.D. BRACKENRIDGE

For Those who have Fallen

Unto Thee, O God, be praise and thanksgiving for all those who have been faithful unto death: into Thy merciful keeping we commend their souls, beseeching Thee to grant unto all of us for whom they died, that their love and devotion may bear fruit in us in more abundant love for others, through Him, who by His death had destroyed death – Thy Son our Lord, Jesus Christ.

ANONYMOUS

For All who Suffer

O God our Father, we bring to you in our prayers those who suffer in body or mind as a result of war, or because of the fear and suspicions that separate nation from nation, race from race, and man from man.

We pray also for all refugees, and for those who have lost wife or husband, children or parents, livelihood, security, or home.

Have mercy upon them, O God, and prosper all who seek to help them in their need, for the sake of Jesus Christ our Lord.

FRANK COLQUHOUN

Strengthen Them, O Lord

O God, who hast promised that they that wait upon thee shall renew their strength, we commend to thee all who suffer in this time of war; the wounded, the sick, and the prisoners; the homeless, the hungry, and the oppressed; the anxious, the frightened, and the bereaved. Strengthen them, O Lord, with thy Holy Spirit, and give them friends to help them; we ask it in his name, who bore for us the agony of the cross, thy Son, our Lord Jesus Christ.

FREDERICK B. MACNUTT

For Those of Ill-Will

O Lord, remember not only the men and women of good will, but also those of ill-will. But do not remember all the suffering they have inflicted on us; remember the fruits we have bought, thanks to this suffering – our comradeship, our loyalty, our humility, our courage, our generosity, the greatness of heart which has grown out of all

this, and when they come to judgement, let all
the fruits which we have borne be their
forgiveness.

ANONYMOUS (IN RAVENSBRUCH
CONCENTRATION CAMP)

Give Peace

Give Peace in our time, O Lord.
Because there is none other that fighteth
for us, but only thou, O God.

THE BOOK OF COMMON PRAYER

Comfort in Sorrow

Not one of us goes through life without suffering the loss of a loved one. The experience, of course, varies according to the relationship we had, what were the circumstances surrounding the death – whether the one who died was elderly and ill for a long time or young and suddenly taken, and also on the type of person we are, and what inner resources we have to cope with our loss.

In the case of intense grief there are some common features of behaviour. A sudden death causes a terrible shock and feeling of unreality. We can't believe it's true; it's like a nightmare from which we long to wake up. We may find ourselves looking for the deceased, or imagining that a knock on the door is his return. There are often feelings of anger and the urge to blame someone, if not for causing the death (which is often the case), then for not doing enough to prevent it – ambulance workers, doctors, hospitals, even God. Strangely, we may even feel angry at our loved one for having left us without warning and in such sorrow. We can be indignant with relatives and friends, and sharp with those who try to help us.

And there are feelings of guilt – perhaps due to a quarrel we never had the chance to make up, or those times during an exhausting period of nursing when we were irritable and said unkind things we never really meant. We feel guilty because we lacked enough sympathy and should have done more, and now these memories come back to haunt us. If only we had a chance to say we are sorry! It's hard to see when our heart is breaking with grief that these feelings, which seem to be so negative, are really expressions of our deep love. One day they will fit into place.

Loneliness is the mother of agonies, and bereavement brings it home like nothing else. Lives that once were intertwined are now severed. The bereaved sometimes say their condition is like an amputation – a part of them is missing. There is now a gap, an emptiness – the empty chair, the empty bed, the empty house we come back to. A widow is no more a wife. 'We' has suddenly become 'I', and 'ours', 'mine'. Jobs that a loved one did or that were done together have now to be done alone, and hands must turn to unfamiliar things. Sadly, to the pain of loneliness is often added the apathy of relatives and friends who forsake us when we need them most, unable perhaps to relate to us in our present distress. Also families today are more scattered than ever, making regular visits difficult, and in many cases impossible.

Grieving is terribly painful, and often lengthy. It can affect us physically, with tightness in the throat, shortness of breath, emptiness in the stomach, loss of weight and loss of sleep. For a while we are in a mental vacuum, with normal life disrupted, and spiritually we can feel at a distance from God. At times we may feel we are losing our minds, and there is a yearning to die and be with our loved one.

Recovery takes time and we cannot be rushed. Tears will play a large part in the process, and we must not be ashamed of them or embarrassed at breaking down in front of others. Suppression of grief can well cause lasting damage. We must try to avoid self-pity, which is destructive of healing and repellent to our family and friends. It is a natural inclination to feel sorry for ourselves, but unchecked it can lead to excessive mourning. So there is a balance to keep. When C.S. Lewis' wife died he went through a period of indulgence in self-pity. When eventually he recovered from mourning her death he realised he could then remember her better. Excessive grief, he believed, does not link us to our dead but cuts us off from them. We do well to set his thoughts before us as a goal to reach.

Meanwhile, we must patiently live through our sorrow, accepting help and friendship when it is offered and needed. It is important to keep up interests in life outside ourselves and our home, and here the Christian Church, with its spiritual teaching and caring fellowship, is of invaluable assistance. One day we may feel better, the next day somewhat worse, but the process of healing has begun. Just as a broken limb needs time to heal, and a festering wound must be cleansed before recovery, so with a broken heart.

Dr Murray Parkes, whose book *Bereavement* has helped an untold number of people, makes a most moving observation out of his vast experience:

In many respects, then, grief can be regarded as an illness. But it can also bring strength. Just as broken bones may end up stronger than unbroken ones, so the experience of grieving can strengthen and bring maturity to those who have previously been protected from misfortune. The pain of grief is just as much a part of life as the joy of love; it is, perhaps, the price we pay for love, the cost of commitment. To ignore this fact, or to pretend that it is not so, is to put on emotional blinkers which leave us unprepared for the losses that will inevitably occur in our lives and unprepared to help others to cope with the losses in theirs.

Grief

How long must I suffer anguish in my soul,
grief in my heart, day and night?

PSALM 13.2 NEB

My life is worn away with sorrow and my years
    with sighing;
strong as I am, I stumble under my load of
    misery.

PSALM 31.10 NEB

Jesus wept.

JOHN 11.35

He will wipe away all tears from their eyes.

REVELATION 21.4 GNB

The Man of Sorrows

Our fellow-sufferer yet retains
A fellow-feeling of our pains,
And still remembers in the skies
His tears, His agonies and cries.

In every pang that rends the heart
The Man of Sorrows has a part;
He sympathizes with our grief,
And to the sufferer sends relief.

SCOTTISH PARAPHRASE BASED ON HEBREWS
4.14–16

Enough Sorrow and Suffering

If we could read the secret history of the world,
we should find in each man's life sorrow and
suffering enough to disarm all hostility.

HENRY WADSWORTH LONGFELLOW

Wounds of The Spirit

There are wounds of the spirit which never close,
and are intended in God's mercy to bring us ever
nearer to him, and to prevent us leaving him, by
their very perpetuity. Such wounds, then, may
almost be taken as a pledge, or at least as a
ground for the humble trust, that God will give
us the great gift of perseverance to the end. . . .

This is how I comfort myself in my own great bereavements.

JOHN HENRY NEWMAN

Longing

But, oh, for the touch of a vanished hand,
And the sound of a voice that is still!

ALFRED LORD TENNYSON

Added to Suffering

I do not believe that sheer suffering teaches. If suffering alone taught, all the world would be wise, since everyone suffers. To suffering must be added mourning, understanding, patience, love, openness and the willingness to remain vulnerable.

ANNE MORROW LINDBERGH

Marooned in Misery

In the teeth of the evidence, I do not believe that any suffering is ultimately absurd or pointless. But it is often difficult to go on convincing oneself. When someone we love dies or meets with a violent accident, when a child is brutally murdered or dies of cancer, when a deep relationship is broken up, or when any disappointment or upheaval strikes, despair may set in. We are marooned in misery. Shaking our fists, pounding the air, we ask that despairing and futile question, why. Why, why, why? Most of all, why ME? What have I done to deserve it? If I were God, I wouldn't allow such awful things to happen. How can there be a God of love when the world is full of suffering? The very idea is a mockery. So we give ourselves two frightful alternatives: either God is cruel, unjust, without mercy, a super-being who delights in the affliction of his creatures; or there is no God and we are adrift in total absurdity, in uncharted and unchartable seas. It's a classic double-bind, a Catch-22 situation. Heads nobody wins, tails we all lose.

MARY CRAIG

Deep Sobbing

Deep sobs –
that start beneath my heart
and hold my body in a grip that hurts.
The lump that swells inside my throat
brings pain that tries to choke.
Then tears course down my cheeks –
I drop my head in my so empty hands
abandoning myself to deep dark grief
and know that with the passing of time
will come relief.
That though the pain may stay
There soon will come a day
When I can say her name and be at peace.

NORAH LENEY

Love in your Sorrow

He is not the least impatient with you for crying;
no, nor for that deep sort of grief which would

like to cry, but the tears will not come. Do not be in a hurry. He loves you *in* your sorrow. He is moved tenderly towards you because of your sorrow. He knows all about it in his own experience.

H.C.G. MOULE

We who are Left

We who are left, how shall we look again
Happily on the sun or feel the rain,
Without remembering how they who went
Ungrudgingly, and spent
Their all for us, loved too the sun and rain?

A bird among the rain-wet lilac sings –
But we, how shall we turn to little things,
And listen to the birds and winds and streams
Made holy by their dreams,
Nor feel the heart-break in the heart of things?

W.W. GIBSON

No Funeral Gloom

No funeral gloom my dears when I am gone,
Corpse-gazing, tears, black raiment, grave-yard
    grimness,
Think of me as withdrawn into the dimness,
Yours still, you mine. Remember all the best
Of our past moments, and forget the rest,
And so, to where I wait, come – gently – on!

ELLEN TERRY

I Would like to Come

Since I lost you, my darling, the sky has come
   near,
And I am of it, the small sharp stars are quite
   near,
The white moon going among them like a white
   bird among snow-berries,
And the sound of her gently rustling in heaven
   like a bird I hear.

And I am willing to come to you now, my dear,
As a pigeon lets itself off from a cathedral dome
To be lost in the haze of the sky; I would like to
   come
And be lost out of sight with you, like a melting
   foam.

For I am tired, my dear, and if I could lift my
   feet,
My tenacious feet, from off the dome of the
   earth
To fall like a breath within the breathing wind
Where you are lost, what rest, my love, what
   rest!

D.H. LAWRENCE

I'm A Widow

Alec was the focal point of my life and I was the
focal point of his, and it was the loss of that
which was the saddest thing of all. It was at the
heart of all my sadness. . . . However good
society is, and however caring and however

marvellous, the actual pain of that separation and that empty place inside me are just mine. No one else can deal with that for me. When the pain is very bad what I try to do is just to be still and feel or react . . . If I want to sit and howl my eyes out then I will. Whatever I feel I want to do I just do it. I don't try to escape.

One of the things Alec used to say was, 'It will pass . . .' Bad times do pass, and that's quite useful to hang on to. It will pass. But I don't want to push it away. I like to stay with it. I don't want to miss out on even the hard and the painful bits. But sometimes it's pretty horrid . . .

PADDY YORKSTONE

The Sun Will Shine Again

I have an updated translation of an Eastern saying pinned by my desk: 'If you want to get rid of the darkness you turn on the light.' In the early days after Peter's death I couldn't bear harsh light. Or loud music. Even the radio or television. It's as if part of you is still lingering on the edge of that other world. You don't want the distractions that will pin you back to earth or inquisitive searchlights probing your innermost secrets. All you can bear is the soft flickering of a candle; a gentle light beside you in the darkness, and equally fragile. Then slowly, imperceptibly, when you have almost given up hope, a faint glimmer of dawn flushes the horizon, bringing with it the gradual realisation that there may be a possibility of new beginnings. The sun will shine again, however many rainbows may temporarily blur your vision – even after three and a half years.

WENDY GREEN

Thank God for Them

Let us thank God for the years they were with us, for the gaiety and happiness, and the companionship and love they gave us. These are things that nothing can take away, they are ours to hold in our hearts and cherish all the days of our lives. Let us dwell on these things, and not on the sadness of a temporary farewell.

ANONYMOUS

Jesus, Man of Tears

Our Jesus is a man of tears. He must have wept a lot. When he heard that Lazarus had died and been removed to a tomb, he wept (John 11.35). It is human to weep. And if we believe that Jesus is God incarnate, then it is also divine to weep. Those who saw Jesus weep for Lazarus said: 'How dearly he must have loved him!' (John, 11.36). Tears mean the capacity for love. Those who have no capacity for love have no tears. It is only when you love deeply, only if you love dearly, that you can weep.

C. S. SONG

All is Well

Death is nothing at all . . . I have only slipped away into the next room. I am I and you are you.

Whatever we were to each other that we are still. Call me by my old familiar name, speak to me in the easy way which you always used. Put no difference in your tone; wear no forced air of solemnity or sorrow. Laugh as we always laughed at the little jokes we enjoyed together. Play, smile, think of me, pray for me. Let my name be ever the household word that it always was. Let it be spoken without effort, without the ghost of a shadow on it. Life means all that it ever meant. It is the same as it ever was; there is absolutely unbroken continuity. Why should I be out of mind because I am out of sight? I am waiting for you for an interval, somewhere very near, just around the corner. All is well.

HENRY SCOTT HOLLAND

Comfort Us Who Mourn

Eternal God,
Lord of life, conqueror of death,
our help in every time of trouble,
comfort us who mourn;
and give us grace, in the presence of death,
to worship you, the ever-living,
so that we may have sure hope of eternal life
and be enabled to put our whole trust
in your goodness and mercy;
through Jesus Christ our Lord.

A BOOK OF SERVICES

God of All Consolation

God of all consolation,
in your unending love and mercy for us
you turn the darkness of death
into the dawn of new life.
Show compassion to your people in their
    sorrow.

Be our refuge and our strength
to lift us from the darkness of this grief
to the peace and light of your presence.

Your son, our Lord Jesus Christ,
by dying for us, conquered death
and by rising again, restored life.

May we then go forward eagerly to meet him,
and after our life on earth
be reunited with our brothers and sisters
where every tear will be wiped away.

PASTORAL CARE OF THE SICK

PART TWO

The Life That We Gain

The death of our loved ones, and the inevitable death that we all face, would be an unspeakable adversity and sadness were it not for our hope in life after death. The Christian faith, in particular, arising out of the death and resurrection of Jesus, meets our highest aspirations.

Jesus Lives, and We Live

Christians find their greatest source of comfort and strength in sorrow in the life and teaching of Jesus, and supremely in his resurrection and promise of eternal life.

His earthly father Joseph had clearly died by the time of Jesus' public ministry, so he would have known sorrow within his own family, and personal loss at quite an early age. He knew what it was like to lose a friend, in this case Lazarus, over whom we are told, 'Jesus wept' (John 11.35), and that brings him so close to us in our sorrow. We find that he mingled with mourners in their homes, and we read of a few occasions when he restored the dead to life.

Jesus talked a great deal about death, though never in a morbid way. He took for granted the fact of natural death and therefore said little about it. He was mainly concerned with what awaited his faithful followers, and to get through to them the significance of his own impending death. He warned his disciples they would die for their faith, but promised that their courage and perseverance would bring them salvation and result in the furtherance of his kingdom. Anyone who chooses to follow him must be ready to 'take up the cross', but such a self-sacrifice would reap its reward (Mark 8.34–5).

Jesus believed his own death would be the fulfilment of his unique calling to surrender his life 'as a ransom for many' (Mark 10.45). It would be as a grain of wheat dying in the soil in order to produce the next harvest (John 12.24).

Several times he repeated the prediction that he would be rejected, put to death, and 'rise again three days afterwards' (Mark 8.31). His resurrection would usher in a new form of life and give a new purpose for living to all who believe. His followers would reap the benefits of his resurrection; they would come from all parts of the world and dine at his great banquet (Matthew 8.11), an implication here of the celebration of his victory and Lordship.

Jesus' resurrection lies at the heart of the New Testament and of the Church's preaching. His disciples met with him several times after Easter morning and before his ascension, and could give personal testimony of his risen presence. The apostle selected to replace Judas was to join the others 'as a witness to his resurrection' (Acts 1.22), and the emphasis of the Pentecost message itself was that Jesus, who had been crucified, was alive again 'as we can all bear witness' (Acts 2.32).

To this day Christianity proudly proclaims the wonder and significance of Christ's resurrection. We affirm in the Apostles' Creed that he was 'crucified, dead and buried . . . the third day he rose again from the dead'. In the risen Lord lies our hope of eternal life after death, and our comfort and support in bearing the sorrows of this life.

Risen Life

Jesus said . . . 'I am the resurrection and the life. Whoever believes in me will live, even though he dies; and whoever lives and believes in me will never die.'

JOHN 11.25–6 GNB

'There are many rooms in my Father's house, and I am going to prepare a place for you . . . I will come back and take you to myself, so that you will be where I am . . . because I live, you also will live.'

JOHN 14.2–3, 19 GNB

We know that God, who raised the Lord Jesus to life, will also raise us up with Jesus and take us . . . into his presence

2 CORINTHIANS 4.14 GNB

And this is what Christ himself promised to give us – eternal life.

1 JOHN 2.25 GNB

(See also: Romans 6.1–11; 8.31–9; 1 Corinthians 15.12–26, 35–58; 2 Corinthians 4.16–18; Philippians 3.12–14; Colossians 3.1–4; Hebrews 12.1–2; 1 Peter 1.3–9; Revelation 14.13; 21.1–7.)

Death in Vain

Vain the stone, the watch, the seal;
Christ hath burst the gates of hell:
Death in vain forbids His rise;
Christ hath opened paradise.

Lives again our glorious King:
Where, O death, is now thy sting?
Once He died, our souls to save:
Where thy victory, O grave?

CHARLES WESLEY

Jesus Lives

In light defeating darkness,
In wisdom conquering foolishness,
In trust overcoming fearfulness,
        Jesus Lives.

In strength coming to weakness,
In health rescuing from sickness,
In hope saving from despair,
        Jesus Lives.

In love victorious over hatred,
In forgiveness dispelling anger,
In glory dispersing drabness,
        Jesus Lives.

In joy growing from sorrow,
In life rising from death,
In God giving the victory,
        Jesus Lives.

He holds the keys of love
                  of peace
He holds the keys of life
                  of death
He holds the keys of heaven
                  of earth
He holds the keys of now
                  of eternity.

DAVID ADAM

On Such a Lovely Morning

In the sky
The song of the skylark
Greets the dawn.
In the fields wet with dew
The scent of the violets
Fills the air.
On such a lovely morning as this
Surely on such a lovely morning as this
Lord Jesus
Came forth
From the tomb.

MISUNO GENZO

Belief in the Resurrection

Belief in the Resurrection is not an appendage to the Christian faith; it is the Christian faith.

We cannot begin to understand how it happened. The Gospels cannot explain the Resurrection; it is the Resurrection which alone explains the Gospels.

J.S. WHALE

Easter Faith

It is the Easter faith, the faith in the risen and living Lord, which makes us able to meet life. For if we believe that Jesus Christ is risen and living, then we must believe that all life is lived in his presence, that we are literally never alone, that we are called upon to make no effort, to endure no sorrow, to face no temptation without him.

It is the Easter faith . . . which makes us able to meet death. It is the Easter faith that we have a friend and a companion who lived and who died and who is alive for ever more, who is the conqueror of death. The presence which is with us in life is with us in death and beyond.

WILLIAM BARCLAY

Written Promise

Our Lord has written the promise of the resurrection not in books alone, but in every leaf in springtime.

MARTIN LUTHER

So We May Trust Thy Love

Grant unto us, O God, to trust thee
    not for ourselves alone
but for those also whom we love
    and who are hid from us
    by the shadow of death;
that, as we believe thy power to have raised
    our Lord Jesus Christ from the dead,

so we may trust thy love
to give eternal life
to all who believe in him;
through the same Jesus Christ our Lord.

GEORGE APPLETON

Lord, Come Alive

Lord, come alive within my experience,
within my sorrows and disappointments and
    doubts,
within the ordinary movements of my life.
Come alive as the peace and joy and assurance
    that is
stronger than the locked doors within, with
    which we try to shut out life.
Come alive as the peace and joy and assurance
    that nothing in life or death can kill.

REX CHAPMAN

Our Hope of Life in Heaven

From the dawn of history man has looked forward to a life after death. Stone Age man buried his dead with tools and cooking utensils. The death rituals of ancient Egypt, Chinese ancestor worship, Hindu belief in the eternal soul or atma, Buddhism's eightfold journey toward Nirvana, Plato's teaching on immortality – all testify to immortal longings. Belief in the survival of the soul after physical death is a universal element in all religions. The funerary rites of his religion have always recognised that man is more than an animal to be cast away with no future, and have accorded him due dignity on his departure.

Is it all wishful thinking, or rather, an inseparable part of our make up and experience of earthly life? Where has the longing come from, and why should we be possessed of it unless there is a satisfactory accomplishment? Do we not glimpse eternity during our sojourn here, when, as the poet Wordsworth believed, 'we see into the heart of things'? There are times when we feel small and insignificant, but more often we know ourselves to be larger than life and born for a destiny beyond death, which alone can fulfil our unfulfilled potential and redress life's inequalities. Immanuel Kant said, 'Man's faculties, desires and earthly gifts reach far beyond earthly use.'

The writer to the Hebrews recognised every man's immortal longings, but spoke as a believer in Christ, whose resurrection is our gateway to life beyond death: 'Here we have no permanent home, but we are seekers after the city which is to come' (Hebrews 13.14 NEB). It is in Christ who died and rose again that our anticipation of the hereafter becomes most hopeful and exciting because, we believe, it will be a life with him in heaven. And since it is 'with him' it can only be a life of unsurpassed quality and pleasure.

In heaven we shall have unlimited opportunity to attain to what Paul calls 'mature manhood, measured by nothing less than the full stature of Christ' (Ephesians 4.13 NEB). And in heaven we shall 'see God'. This is known as the 'beatific vision', and derives from Revelation 22.3–4: 'The throne of God and of the Lamb will be there, and his servants shall worship him; they shall see him face to face' (NEB). These words are echoed in our Lord's beatitude, 'How blest are those whose hearts are pure; they shall see God' (Matthew 5.8 NEB).

Hope Alive

Those who hope for no other life are dead even for this.

JOHANN WOLFGANG VON GOETHE

Eternal Spring

Winter is on my head but eternal spring is in my heart. The nearer I approach the end, the plainer I hear around me the immortal symphonies of the world to come. For half a century I have been writing my thoughts in prose and verse; but I feel that I have not said one-thousandth part of what is in me. When I have gone down to the grave I shall have ended my day's work; but another day will begin the next morning. Life closes in the twilight but opens with the dawn.

VICTOR HUGO

The Sea has Another Shore

The man of faith may face death as Columbus faced his first voyage from the shores of Spain. What lies beyond the seas he cannot tell: all his special expectations may be mistaken, but his insight into the clear meaning of present facts may persuade him beyond doubt that the sea has another shore.

H.E. FOSDICK

As the Seed

A seed dies into a new life, and so does man.

GEORGE MACDONALD

Into Eternity

The days, the years, the hours,
Are they a quagmire?

Sucking us down, from birth
To our inevitable death;
Or could they lead, step by step
Into Eternity?
Has God, or the Nothing that set creation going,
Planned this tragic mockery,
This mad charade, of going down to death?
Is all nothing and in the end,
Nothing, all?

Or was Christ right?
God giving us bread and not a stone,
A fish and not a serpent?
Eternal life, not the black voidal horror
Of the grave?

JOAN BROCKELSBY

Heaven is God

Heaven is God, and God is in my soul.

ELISABETH DE LA TRINITÉ

Carry Me Home

I looked over Jordan, and what did I see,
Coming for to carry me home?
A band of angels coming after me,
Coming for to carry me home.

Swing low, sweet chariot,
Coming for to carry me home,
Swing low, sweet chariot,
Coming for to carry me home.

If you get there before I do,
Coming for to carry me home,
Tell all my friends I'm coming too,
Coming for to carry me home.

I'm sometimes up, I'm sometimes down,
Coming for to carry me home,
But still my soul feels heavenly bound,
Coming for to carry me home.

AFRICAN-AMERICAN SPIRITUAL

Where I Live by Sight

I have formerly lived by hear-say and faith, but
now I go where I shall live by sight, and shall be
with him in whose company I delight myself.

JOHN BUNYAN

As Strangers Here

Saints by the power of God are kept,
    Till the salvation come;
We walk by faith as strangers here,
    But Christ shall call us home.

ISAAC WATTS

He Shall Suffice Me

Yea, through life, death, through sorrow and
    through sinning
He shall suffice me, for he hath sufficed;
Christ is the end, for Christ was the beginning,
Christ the beginning, for the end is Christ.

FREDERIC W. MYERS

Heavenly Vision

Bring us, O Lord God, at the last awakening into the house and gate of heaven, to enter into that gate and dwell in that house, where there shall be no darkness nor dazzling, but one equal light; no noise nor silence, but one equal music; no fears nor hopes, but one equal possession; no ends nor beginnings, but one equal eternity, in the habitations of thy majesty and thy glory, world without end.

JOHN DONNE

Shall I One Day See Thee?

O my God, shall I one day see thee? What sight can compare to that great sight? Shall I see the source of that grace which enlightens me, strengthens me, and consoles me? As I came from thee, as I am made through thee, so. O my God, may I at last return to thee, and be with thee for ever and ever.

JOHN HENRY NEWMAN

Begin Heaven on Earth

O God of patience and consolation, grant we beseech thee that with free hearts we may love and serve thee and our brethren; and, having thus the mind of Christ, may begin heaven on earth, and exercise ourselves therein till that day when heaven, where love abideth, shall seem no strange habitation to us; for Jesus Christ's sake.

CHRISTINA ROSSETTI

In Heaven to See Thy Face

Lord Jesus, give us grace
　　On earth to love thee more,
In heaven to see thy face,
　　And with thy saints adore.

WILLIAM BULLOCK
HENRY WILLIAMS BAKER

Reunited in Love

I am ceaselessly grateful to have been blessed with a happy marriage and a wife whom I love dearly. As I look forward in faith to the hereafter I naturally hope that our love for each other will continue, for I cannot imagine complete happiness without her.

Should we expect a continuation in the next life of the relationships we formed in this one? I believe so. We are reminded, of course, that when Jesus was asked about the after-life relationships of a woman who had been married seven times, 'Whose wife will she be?', he answered that at the resurrection 'men and women do not marry; they are like angels in heaven' (Mark 12.25 NEB). It was a cynical question from the Sadducees who, as we know, did not believe in the resurrection of the dead. Jesus' reply showed how inappropriate it is to think of human relationships in heaven in excactly the same way as we have known them here on earth. The resurrection ushers in a new order of living in which the old laws of physical life are transformed. Life in heaven is of a new dimension and hitherto unknown experience.

It is good to have this larger vision. However fulfilling are our earthly relationships, they are never perfect and are often hindered by obstacles and restricted by our impositions. The resurrection releases our limitations as we become completely part of an ever growing community of love.

But does this mean that our close personal ties, as within marriage, lose their intimacy as they dissipate in a general and all-embracing love for an innumerable company? Surely not. In heaven, whilst our love will be limitless, it will not be less than we have known on earth. Not less, but more. There our broken relationships will be mended, and the ties that bound us until severed by death, will be re-joined and strengthened.

Charles Kingsley's wife is said to have erected over his grave a white marble cross with the inscription, 'We have loved; we love; we shall love', and above it, encircling a cross, the words, 'God is love.'

Our hope and trust lie in God's love. It is worth noting the full text of that supreme assertion: 'God is love, and whoever lives in love lives in union with God and God lives in union with him' (1 John 4.16 GNB). If, as we believe, he wills the love relationship of marriage, the bond between parents and their children, and those of our close friendships, what sort of God would he be to allow death to destroy them for ever, or to disallow their continuation in the next life he has prepared for us? Surely not the loving Father whom Jesus revealed to us. Why such an emphasis in the Bible on the love of God for each of us and our obligation to love one another if love ends at death, or we fail to recognise our loved ones in the hereafter?

We say in the marriage service, 'Those whom God has joined together, let no man separate.' How much more will God see to it that the bonds we have known, not just in marriage, but between us and all who are so dear to us, remain intact? Paul, in his magnificent 'Hymn of Love' (1 Corinthians 13) said that love, alongside faith and hope, lasts for ever, stressing that love, being the greatest, 'will never come to an end'.

For Ever and Always

'Death' does not mean the end of all life, but actually, on the contrary, a birth, a passing over into a new life, a glorious and everlasting life. Hence death is not a fearful thing. It is the separation that is hard, and heavy to bear. But it becomes less hard and less heavy to bear when we remain mindful that we are indeed not parting for ever, but *only for a time* – as for a journey – in order afterwards to meet again *for ever and always* in a life that is infinitely more beautiful than the present one, and that then *there will be no end* of our being together. Remember all this and your burden will surely become lighter.

ALEXANDER SCHMORELL

Life in the Lord

Those who live in the Lord never see each other for the last time.

A PROVERB

As Face to Face

He is not dead, this friend, not dead,
But, in the path we mortals tread,
Got some few, trifling steps ahead
    And nearer to the end;
So that you too, once past the bend,
Shall meet again, as face to face,
    This friend you fancy dead.

ROBERT LOUIS STEVENSON

To Die for Each Other

None can be eternally united who have not died
for each other.

COVENTRY PATMORE

Unbreakable Love

I want to meet again those I have known and
loved, who before they 'died' helped me by their
friendship and encouragement. If God is love as
Jesus taught, then love is eternal, and a relationship of love cannot be broken by physical death.

GEORGE APPLETON

With Our Loved Ones

I love thee with a love I seemed to lose
With my lost saints – I love thee with the breath,
Smiles, tears, of all my life! – and, if God choose,
I shall but love thee better after death.

ELIZABETH BARRETT BROWNING

Together Always

You were born together and together you shall
    be for evermore
You shall be together when the white wings of
    death scatter your days,
Aye, you shall be together even in the silent
    memory of God.

KAHLIL GIBRAN

Inspired by their Example

Almighty God, we beseech thee that, inspired by
the example of thy saints, we may run with
patience the race that is set before us, looking
unto Jesus, the author and finisher of our faith;
so that, when this mortal life is ended, we may be
gathered with those whom we have loved, in the
kingdom of thy glory, where there shall be no
more death, neither sorrow nor crying, neither
shall there be any more pain, for the former
things are passed away; through Jesus Christ our
Lord. Amen.

A BOOK OF SERVICES AND PRAYERS

Lift Our Eyes to that Day

O Lord, we miss our loved ones so much that we
want to be near them. Yet you have risen from
the grave and assured us of their happiness. Forgive us the lack of faith which takes our memory
back to the sad day of parting. Lift our eyes to
that day when we shall meet again in Jesus Christ
our Lord.

IAN D. BUNTING

The Great Communion

A clergyman returned home from an early morning church service at which there had been only six communicants. His wife expressed sadness that so few had attended, but he was not disappointed: 'True, there were only six that we could see, but when we prayed, "Therefore with angels and archangels, and with all the company of heaven, we laud and magnify thy holy name", I was reminded of all the others.'

All Saints' Day on November 1st is a reminder each year of 'all the others' – the countless number of 'saints, apostles, prophets, martyrs' who make up the church redeemed and triumphant in heaven.

In his vision of that church, John, the writer of the Book of Revelation, told of a crowd, too large to be counted, standing before God and offering their worship (7.9–10). In remembering the ever expanding company of the faithful in heaven, and rejoicing in the spiritual fellowship of the Communion of the Saints, we realise how truly great the church is.

The day following All Saints is All Souls, set aside for the commemoration of the faithful departed. It is very much a personal festival when we recall and give thanks for those whom we have 'loved and lost awhile', but who too are part of the Church Triumphant in heaven. It's an occasion for everyone, for all of us know the pain of parting brought about by the death of loved ones.

We don't, of course, have to wait for just one or two days in the year on which to remember and hold communion with them; they and we are part of each other at all times, bonded together in the love of God in which prayer for each other is a lifeline. In fact, there is no need for us to attempt any other contact with them – prayer alone, within the orbit of God's love, is sufficient.

One Family, One Church

Let saints below in concert sing
    With those to glory gone;
For all the servants of our King
    In earth and heaven are one.

One family we dwell in Him,
    One Church, above, beneath,
Though now divided by the stream,
    The narrow stream of death.

CHARLES WESLEY

Joined in Prayer

The saints, because they are closer to God now than when they were on earth, share even more intimately in his work. Part of that work is interceding for people according to Christ's will. We can, if we want, ask for the prayers of the saints in general or one saint in particular. We have friends on earth and sometimes we ask one of them to pray for us. We also have friends in heaven and it is just as natural to ask them to pray for us. It no more takes away from the centrality of Christ and his grace than asking an earthly friend to pray for us. All prayer, whether on earth or in heaven, is Christ praying in and through us.

It is just as natural to pray for the departed. More often than now happens, our prayers should express thanks. We should remember with gratitude particular aspects of the life and character of someone we have loved and give thanks to God for them. But this prayer can also include the request that the loved one be drawn ever deeper into God. The traditional words, 'Rest eternal grant unto them, O Lord. Let light perpetual shine upon them', have a never fading truth and beauty.

RICHARD HARRIES

A Crossing the World

They that love beyond the world cannot be separated by it. Death is but a crossing the world, as friends do the seas; they live in one another still.

WILLIAM PENN

One In Christ

Each human being belongs not only to that part of humanity which, living on earth at the moment, stands before God in prayer and labour, for the present generation is only a page in the book of life. In God and in his church there is no difference between living and dead, and all are one in the love of the Father. Even the generations yet to be born are part of this one divine humanity.

SERGIUS BULGAKOV

Remember our Brothers and Sisters

Lord, remember in mercy your Church throughout the world; make all its members to grow in love for you and for one another.

Remember our brothers and sisters who have gone to their rest in the hope of the resurrection to eternal life; and bring us with them into the light of your presence, that in union with all your saints we may give you glory for ever, through your Son Jesus Christ our Lord.

ADAPTED FROM
A ROMAN CATHOLIC REQUIEM

United to Thyself

O Lord our God, from whom neither life nor death can separate those who trust in thy love, and whose love holds in its embrace thy children in this world and the next; so unite us to thyself that in fellowship with thee we may always be united to our loved ones whether here or there; give us courage, constancy and hope; through him who died and was buried and rose again for us, Jesus Christ our Lord.

WILLIAM TEMPLE

The Unseen Cloud of Witnesses

Eternal God, help us always to remember the great unseen cloud of witnesses round about us. When in danger, give us their courage and when in difficulty, their perseverance; so that we too may be faithful until we rejoice with all the saints in your eternal kingdom, through Jesus Christ our Lord. Amen.

WILLIAM HAMPSON

PART THREE

The Faith that we Need: Losses other than death

Whatever our gains and successes in this life, we also suffer a variety of losses and failures. These affect us in one way or another, and require that we hold them in perspective and meet them with faith.

Health Diminished

Good physical health is a priceless blessing. Some of us are fortunate to have it from birth and to continue bodily fit for many years. I knew a man of eighty-two who went into hospital for a minor operation, and for the first time in his life. He never lost a day's work through illness, and had to think hard when he last needed to see his doctor. In contrast I have known scores of other unfortunate ones who have always been dogged with ill health, and are often in constant pain.

Quite commonly the good health we have enjoyed breaks down, either suddenly or gradually, leaving us impeded and distressed. Stanley, aged sixty-six, seemed a fit man when he retired twelve months ago, and he looked forward to several years of enjoyment doing some of the things he'd longed to do in his own time. Suddenly he suffered a stroke that has severely reduced his physical faculties, and he fights pain and frustration daily. He is one of countless individuals, past and present, who bear the burden of illness, and to whom our hearts go out in compassion.

'Look to your health,' said Izaak Walton; 'and if you have it, praise God, and value it next to a good conscience; for health is the second blessing that we mortals are capable of; a blessing that money cannot buy.'

Sickness and Pain

Be merciful to me, O Lord, for I am weak.

PSALM 6.2 NEB

Consider my distress and suffering.

PSALM 25.18 GNB

Even though our physical being is gradually decaying, yet our spiritual being is renewed day after day.

2 CORINTHIANS 4.16 GNB

Suffering First-Hand

Suffering is an initiation into human experience which we can never know at second-hand. No matter how much we read or hear of what others have to say about it, there is something that cannot be imparted. Perhaps that was one reason why Plato said that a physician should not be a man who has always enjoyed robust health. It is only by your own suffering that you are admitted to the fellowship of pain.

LESLIE TIZARD

A Long Pain

An hour of pain is as long as a day of pleasure.

ENGLISH PROVERB

Without Suffering

If I had not suffered
I would not have known the love of God.
If many people had not suffered
God's love would not have been passed on.
If Jesus had not suffered
God's love would not have been made visible.

MIZUNO GENZO

I Wrote It

Once my father went to see a girl who had had a long illness and who was quite helpless. She would never walk again, and all that she had to look forward to was a slow and lingering death. He took with him a little book of Christian comfort, a book radiant with certainty and with joy. He gave it to her, saying: 'I thought that you might like to have this book.' She took it and looked at it and smiled. Then she said shyly: 'I wrote it.'

WILLIAM BARCLAY

Painful Prayers

The best prayers have often more groans than words.

JOHN BUNYAN

Learning Through Suffering

To have suffered much is like knowing many languages. Thou hast learned to understand all.

GEORGE ELIOT

Scars to Show

God will not look you over for medals, degrees or diplomas, but for scars!

ELBERT HUBBARD

A Gift

In the last few months of his life, Joyce Cary, the writer, was so crippled with paralysis that he could no longer speak. He was unable to dictate, and the only means of communicating that was left to him was laborious writing with a pen tied to his hand.

One day he wrote, 'I look upon life as a gift from God. I did nothing to earn it. Now that the time is coming to give it up, I have no right to complain.'

FROM *A NEW DAY*, COMPILED BY D.M. PRESCOTT

Life Worth Living

Crying is all right and you have got to do it sometimes. If you feel as if you have got to cry, please do, but don't do it all the time. There is one thing to remember above all, you have only one life so try to make the most of it. I'd just like to say don't give in, there is a lot to life, there is a lot worth living for in it. I know that because I'm going to be a dancer.

JOANNE GILLESPIE (AGED 9)

Suffering With Us

The New Testament teaching on suffering takes it into an entirely different sphere. Our Lord is not standing by seeing how we get on; he is actually suffering with us. Our pain is his pain, our swollen useless limbs are his; but, ultimately, our weakness becomes his strength and our defeat becomes his victory. Here lies one more, and surely the most profound, truth about suffering: it enables us to identify most closely with our Lord.

JAMES CASSON

At the Foot of the Cross

What is the meaning of pain? How does it find a place in a world created by a loving God? . . . At the foot of the Cross, we learn once for all that pain – agonising pain – may find a place in the perfect life. It did have place there. The perfect life and death were sinless; they were not painless.

On the contrary, the pain directly contributed to the perfection of the life and death. It was in the endurance of the pain that the supreme courage was perfected; it was in the selfless endurance of pain that the supreme love was perfected. Take away pain from life, and you take heroism with it: the result is to make life poorer, not richer.

WILLIAM TEMPLE

Filled With His Presence

Jesus did not come to explain suffering nor to take it away: he came to fill it with his presence.

PAUL CLAUDEL

Refuge and Repose

Teach us, O Lord, to know our frailty, that we may find our refuge and repose in thy eternal changelessness.

J.H. OLDHAM

The Pain is Still There

I hurt again, Lord,
I hurt all over.
From the very onset of my sickness I rebelled against pain,
I hid behind my medicine bottles,
I threw myself at you in what must have been pure melodrama, begging a reprieve.
Yet somehow you must have seen something valuable about pain because it is still there.
I suppose I should be thankful, but I'm not very heroic,
I can't smile with gratitude when my body is on the torture rack.
All I ask, Lord, is that you help me grasp the worth of the hurt twisting inside me, because if I knew that, maybe I'd be able to bear up better, maybe then I wouldn't be so cranky with those I love most.
But no matter what, Lord, just help me to get through today without being too much of a burden.

MAX PAULI

For All in Pain

Grant, O Lord, to all those who are bearing pain,
thy spirit of healing, thy spirit of peace and hope,
of courage and endurance. Cast out from them
the spirit of anxiety and fear; grant them perfect
confidence and trust in thee, that in thy light
they may see light; through Jesus Christ our
Lord.

GEORGE APPLETON

Father, Jesus, Spirit

Father of all, who loves each life created,
Hear now our prayers for all distressed and sad,
Whose bodies' weakness leads to minds
    frustrated,
And thoughts are often of a strength they had.

Jesus, who in compassion healed the broken,
The sick, the deaf and dumb, the blind and lame;
Receive our prayers, the silent and the spoken,
For whom your healing touch is sought again.

Spirit of peace, bring soothing calm and coolness
To all who seek you in their anxious need;
Use all whose skill is offered for their wholeness,
Bless healed and healer in this gracious deed.

DAVID M. OWEN

Comfort and Succour

Comfort and succour all those, who in this transitory life are in trouble, sorrow, need, sickness, or any other adversity.

BOOK OF COMMON PRAYER

At Evening

Watch, dear Lord,
with those who wake, or watch, or weep tonight,
and give your angels charge over those who
    sleep.
Tend your sick ones, O Lord Christ,
rest your weary ones.
Bless your dying ones.
Soothe your suffering ones.
Pity your afflicted ones.
Shield your joyous ones.
And all for your love's sake.

ST AUGUSTINE OF HIPPO

loved ones and friends to keep us company...
cannot secure, but we can hope, and in our
hoping and waiting, enjoy a number of those we love
and who love us.

Age Wearied

I read of a teacher of eighty who sends birthday
cards to his friends when they reach sixty, with
this message pinned inside: 'You have spent sixty
years in preparation for life; you will now begin
to live. . . . Danger is past, the mind is peaceful,
evil is forgiven, the affections are strong, envy is
weak. It is the happy age.'

It is a characteristic of old age that as the body
grows weaker, the spirit often grows stronger.

Luke tells us of two such people. There was
Simeon, described as a good and devout man
who, with the wisdom of the years and the habit
of spiritual watchfulness, was able to see in the
child Jesus God's promised Messiah. The proph-
etess Anna, eighty-four years old, was, by that
same devotion, also able to see the truth about
Jesus (Luke 2.25–38).

Together they represent both the potential of
every one of us, and that time of quiet trust and
hopefulness.

Sadly, old age is not that happy an experience
for everyone, nor is the mind always peaceful.
Frailty of body too often steals one's cherished
independence, and brings indignity and
embarrassment.

Most of us would like to live into old age,
provided life retains its good quality and we have

loved ones and friends to keep us company. We cannot be sure, but we can hope, and in our hoping and waiting be mindful of those of whom old age has taken its toll.

In Old Age I will Carry You

. . . And when white hairs come, I will carry you
   still;
I have made you and I will bear the burden.

ISAIAH 46.4 NEB

Despise no man for being old;
some of us are growing old as well.

ECCLESIASTICUS 8.6 NEB

No wonder we do not lose heart! Though our outward humanity is in decay, yet day by day we are inwardly renewed.

2 CORINTHIANS 4.16 NEB

Turn to Gold

The pale leaf turns in pallor,
But the green leaf turns to gold;
We that have found it good to be young
Shall find it good to be old.

G.K. CHESTERTON

Inwardly Stronger

I have been very near to the gates of death, and have returned very weak and an old man, feeble and tottering, but not in the spirit and life, not in the real man, the imagination which liveth for ever. In that I am stronger and stronger, as this foolish body decays.

WILLIAM BLAKE

Enriching the Years

How is it that some people in old age are sweet and lovable, uncomplaining and unselfish, while others are cantankerous and self-pitying, and very difficult to bear with? Probably age accentuates in each of us what we have been all along. Nevertheless, we can help older people, just as we can help our children and each other, to be their finest, and sweetest, and best. We must understand them, their need for things to do that are within their capacity, their need for companionship and someone to talk to. We must love them, simply and warmly. I have seen an old lady utterly transformed by love and understanding from a sour and crabby introvert into a smiling and gracious personality. But where these gifts are costly and difficult to give, God can still provide us with the daily grace to give them.

HELEN R. LEE

Old and Lovely

Let me grow lovely, growing old:
So many old things do.
Laces, and ivory, and gold
Need not be new.

There is healing in old trees;
Old streets a glamour hold.
Why should not I as well as these
Grow lovely, growing old?

WYNFORD G. WHITTAKER

Still Learning

And when youth's gone
As men count going, 'twixt us two alone
Still let me be
Thy little child, left learning at thy knee.

ANONYMOUS

Love and Hope

It is not the years that make souls grow old, but
having nothing to love.

FATHER CONGREVE

Being Old

Yes, my body is old
But it's not the real me.
The real me
Is as young as you are.
In fact, the real me
Never changes.

Yes, I'm trapped in a body
That won't obey me.
But don't let it fool you.
I'm aware of everything around me
And I want to be included.
So don't look at me with pity
Or talk to me as you would a child.
Please don't make me feel useless
Or ignore me.
I have not changed
– not really.
Time has just taken its toll.
The real me is just like you,
With a need to be recognised
And accepted

So be patient with me
If I am a little muddled
Or deaf,
Or need a strong arm to lean on.
For inside I'm flying –
Free and young and mobile.
Please . . .
Try to see me
As I really am.

CAROLYN HOOPER

Beautiful Old Age

It ought to be lovely to be old
to be full of the peace that comes of experience
and wrinkled ripe fulfilment.

The wrinkled smile of completeness that follows
  a life
lived undaunted and unsoured with accepted
  lies.
If people lived without accepting lies
they would ripen like apples, and be scented like
  pippins
in their old age.

Soothing, old people should be, like apples
when one is tired of love.
Fragrant like yellow leaves, and dim with the soft
stillness and satisfaction of autumn.

And a girl should say:
It must be wonderful to live and grow old.
Look at my mother, how rich and still she is! –

And a young man should think: By Jove
my father has faced all weathers, but it's been a
  life!

D.H. LAWRENCE

More Patient and Loving

I hate all this giving up, Lord. I used to be young
and strong and now I'm getting older and can do
less. I know this is bound to be so but I hate it. I
get jealous of young people, cross that I can't
read without glasses, annoyed when I can't hear,
hurt when I am ignored. And I know it will be
worse and life will perhaps be lonelier and emp-
tier! Now I don't want just to grumble, Lord,
because there is a lot of love about and care and

kindness. But I even hate people being kind to me. How silly can I be? Will you help me to be more patient and loving?

MICHAEL HOLLINGS & ETTA GULLICK

Not Easy to Accept

Jesus, who never grew old, it is not easy for any of us to face old age. It is fine to be young, attractive, strong. Old age reminds us of weakness and dependence upon others. But to be your disciple means accepting weakness and inter-dependence. Because of you we can rejoice in weakness in ourselves, and be tender to it in others.

MONICA FURLONG

Faculties Impaired

Edith, seventy-eight, has lost her memory. Her inability to recall the precious happenings of her life and to communicate with her husband and two daughters causes them great sadness. She lives in a world of her own that they cannot enter. George, who is eighty-seven, remembers much about the 1914–18 war in which he was wounded, but can't remember his daughter's visit two days ago. Dorothy is only seventy-four, but already Alzheimer's Disease is taking its dreadful hold on her mind, and she does peculiar things, much to the distress of her husband.

Tony, fifty-three, lost the sight of his right eye in a car accident fifteen years ago; now he's been told his other eye is failing. He loves life, enjoys reading, model-making and watching television, and the likelihood of blindness causes him great concern.

Megan, in her seventies, has lived in a silent world since childhood, when an illness took away her hearing. She has had many years to adjust to her loss, and lives cheerfully, always eager to help others. Still, she says, it would be lovely to hear music and bird song, and to be part of people's conversation in the normal way.

All these have one thing in common, though

each condition varies – their precious faculties of memory, sight and hearing are impaired and their quality of life reduced. Some are born impaired, others are afflicted in the course of life through illness or accident. They are the world's handicapped, but how often have we known the blind and the deaf to rise above their misfortune with courage and initiative that puts the rest of us to shame?

You Know what I Long for

O Lord . . .
I am bowed down, I am crushed;
I mourn all day long . . .
O Lord, you know what I long for;
you hear all my groans.
My heart is pounding,
my strength is gone,
and my eyes have lost their brightness . . .
I am like a deaf man and cannot hear . . .
But I trust in you, O Lord.

PSALM 38 (SELECTED VERSES)

A Kept Memory

Oh, better than the minting
Of a gold-crowned king
Is the safe-kept memory
Of a lovely thing.

SARA TEASDALE

Forgetting

We have all forgot more than we remember.

THOMAS FULLER

Yet Will I Remember Thee

Can a woman's tender care
Cease towards the child she bare?
Yes, she may forgetful be,
Yet will I remember thee.

WILLIAM COWPER

Hardships of Blindness

It's difficult to imagine the problems faced by blind people when you are sighted. Closing your eyes is not enough . . . for being unable to see is just one of many problems they have to face each and every day – disorientation, fear, depression, and tiredness are just some of the others. Many blind people are extremely courageous and learn to overcome these problems with great determination.

For many blind people the loneliness and difficulties of living without sight are overwhelming. Even the smallest everyday tasks, like cooking and washing, can be so very difficult for a blind person to cope with. Too many are struggling in a dark, cold and cheerless world.

NEWSLETTER FOR THE
LONDON ASSOCIATION FOR THE BLIND

How My Light is Spent

When I consider how my light is spent,
Ere half my days, in this dark world and wide,
And that one talent which is death to hide
Lodged with me useless, though my soul more
   bent
To serve therewith my Maker, and present
My true account, lest he returning chide,
'Doth God exact day-labour, light denied?'
I fondly ask. But Patience, to prevent
That murmur, soon replies: 'God doth not need
Either man's work or his own gifts; who best
Bear his mild yoke, they serve him best. His state
Is kingly: thousands at his bidding speed,
And post o'er land and ocean without rest;
They also serve who only stand and wait.'

JOHN MILTON

'Hearing' Music

It didn't disappoint me to learn that no surgery
or hearing aid currently available was going to
restore me to good hearing. I had learnt to cope
with my silent world, and felt that my own ways
of listening to music gave me a sensitivity that I
far preferred to the 'normal' way of hearing that
I had experienced as a tiny child. Because I had
to concentrate with every fibre of my body and
brain, I experienced music with a profundity that
I felt was God-given and precious. I didn't want
to lose that special gift.

   . . . If I have been an inspiration, I am delight-
ed; if I can encourage others to believe in their

121

ability to overcome difficulties and to go for what they want, it is a great joy, and I feel privileged to be in a position where I am able to communicate with so many people, to let them share my optimism about life's possibilities.

EVELYN GLENNIE

Fading Memory

Lord, I fear I'm losing my memory. It's more than just those forgetful lapses that we all have and usually laugh off. I know it's more serious because once-vivid occasions in my life are growing vaguer, and I'm doing and saying silly things. Please help me, and at all costs, let me never be mindless of your loving care and peaceful presence.

DAVID M. OWEN

Losing Sight

O God,
It is hard to think of a world
   in which I cannot see the sun and the flowers,
   and the faces of those I love.
It is hard to think of a life
   in which I cannot read or watch things,
    or see lovely things any more.
But even in the dark there will be something left.
I can still have memory,
   and I can still see things again
   with my mind's eye.
I thank you for Braille, which keeps the world of
   books from being altogether closed to me.

I thank you that I will still be able to hear the
voices I know and to touch the things and
people I love.
Lord Jesus, you are the Light of Life;
Be with me in the dark.

WILLIAM BARCLAY

Going Deaf

I used to hear so well and loved what I heard,
human voices, music, birds, the sound of trains.
Now I'm in a silent world, Lord. People shout at
me and grow cross when I don't hear. It embar-
rasses and hurts me and I cannot now enjoy
music or nature or anything with my hearing. I
pray I may accept it more and learn to use it.

MICHAEL HOLLINGS & ETTA GULLICK

Relationships Broken

My job as a clergyman brings me in daily touch with the traumas of broken relationships, from petty happenings or differences of opinion resulting in the angry word and soured friendship, to marital breakdown that leaves a shattered partner and bewildered children. Some relationships are mended, though scars remain of broken trust; others are severed completely, often with lasting recriminations. Some are compensated for in other ways, others leave an unfulfilled and permanent loneliness.

Life for each of us from beginning to end is an exercise in human relationships. Desert island solitariness is a rare and mostly unwelcomed experience, for we are gregarious creatures needing mutual support and companionship. I have always liked the Authorised Version rendering of Psalm 68 verse 6: 'God setteth the solitary in families.' He might have added, 'even though in families relationships are broken', for it's doubtful whether family life was that harmonious in those far off days!

Each relationship we form is also a human adventure, some would say a gamble, involving the giving of ourselves and our willingness to receive. Both are risky enterprises.

Love and trust are two essential ingredients if

a relationship is to work, but all too often they are missing. Love enables us to put the other person's needs first, to be understanding and tolerant, to keep open the door of reconciliation when disagreements occur. And trust means complete openness and honesty in conversation, and integrity in behaviour, without which no relationship can thrive. Human bonding is the most difficult, but most rewarding of all our endeavours.

Love your Neighbour as Yourself

The man who fears the Lord keeps his friendships in repair, for he treats his neighbour as himself.

ECCLESIASTICUS 6.17 NEB

Do not let sunset find you nursing your anger.

EPHESIANS 4.26 REB

God is love; he who dwells in love is dwelling in God, and God in him.

1 JOHN 4.16 NEB

Indescribably Hurt

John had been cool and unpleasant towards me for about a month, but assured me nothing was wrong. I began to have fearful suspicions. And

125

then the dreaded news broke when he phoned from the office to say he wasn't coming home that night. I said, 'John, I'm terrified you might be leaving me.' He replied stunningly, 'Yes, you're right, I am.' He hung up. For weeks I felt as if I was going out of my mind. I loathed him yet loved him. Having him in the house but not his affection left me indescribably hurt. Divorce severed our marriage at last – that was two years ago, and still I am wounded. Were it not for my Christian faith and the support of my church friends, among others, I don't think I could have made it to this day.

ANONYMOUS, 1991

Marriage Build-up

Marriage is a struggle for adjustment, an experiment in unselfishness, an adventure in self-sacrifice, and oddly enough we must often sacrifice our happiness in order to have any happiness worth having. It is a discipline in kindness, sympathy, renunciation, and utter devotion, not to oneself, but to another, else it fails.

JOSEPH FORT NEWTON

Me, a Neighbour

My neighbour's unloveliness may be the consequence of my unneighbourliness.

WERNER AND LOTTE PELZE

Slow to Quick

Slow to suspect – quick to trust,
Slow to condemn – quick to justify,
Slow to offend – quick to defend,
Slow to expose – quick to shield,
Slow to reprimand – quick to forebear.
Slow to belittle – quick to appreciate,
Slow to demand – quick to serve,
Slow to provoke – quick to conciliate,
Slow to hinder – quick to help,
Slow to resent – quick to forgive.

ANONYMOUS

Love's Desire

Love between persons means that each wants the
other to be more himself.

M.C. D'ARCY

Your Loneliness

Pray that your loneliness may spur you into
finding something to live for, great enough to die
for.

DAG HAMMARSKJÖLD

God as Friend

He loses nothing that keepeth God for his
friend.

THOMAS FULLER

I am my Parents (prayer by a child of a broken marriage)

I know that the pain continues to live in me,
    and that it will never die.
I am willing to be a child
    torn in two,
    split into pieces
    and bleeding.
    For now I know who I am, Lord.

I am the place where they met.
I am the indissoluble link that bonds them
    together.
I am the flesh that cannot be destroyed.
I am their love, which lives so long as I live.
I am they, united for ever in marriage.

Lord, I want to live, so that they may live;
    to grow, so that they may grow;
    to love, so that they may love.
And, in silence, I will beget my parents,
    I will give them life,
    I will help them to grow.
I will save them, in saving their love.

MICHEL QUOIST

Family Estrangement

Heavenly Father, whose will it is that your children should live in peace with you and in harmony with one another: look with compassion on the members of this family now suffering the pain of estrangement.

Give to all a desire for reconciliation;
remove every hindrance to true love and understanding;
and grant that they may find the joy of forgiving and being forgiven, even as they seek your own gracious pardon, through the merits of Jesus Christ our Redeemer.

MARTIN PARSONS

Stand with Us

Lord Jesus, you knew what it was to be alone;
to realise that no one else shared your vision
and that no one would stand with you;
to be deserted by all your friends;
even to doubt the presence of God.

If you could know such despair,
what chance of escape is there for us?
Stand with us in our times of need,
   when we are afraid,
   when we are full of grief,
   when we have taken the wrong path,
   and when we have hurt those we love most.
Stand with us that we may know that we are never alone.

MORE EVERYDAY PRAYERS

Faith Weakened

Arthur has long been a practising Christian, but when his wife died following a long and painful illness, and shortly afterwards his daughter gave birth to a Down's syndrome baby, he confessed: 'This double tragedy has really damaged my faith. I'm trying not to give up on God, but I hope I'll find reassurance soon.'

Janice has been brought up in a Christian home and through a caring church, but half way through her college course her faith began to wane. She admits that her many other interests had something to do with it, and that she left off going to church, but also she found her once-held beliefs losing their relevance and strength of conviction.

Some of our doubts are dishonest – mere smokescreens we imagine will hide us from God when we are really too busy to concern ourselves with him. We can be sure he sees through these. On the other hand, honest doubts in the face of personal trial or intellectual persuasion, are surely met with gentleness and understanding. In this case God waits patiently, and in his waiting, loves us as much as ever, and longs, like the father of the Prodigal, to welcome us home.

To have faith in God is not to withdraw into a problem-free zone where all his ways are clearly revealed and no questions are asked. This would be to deny in us his gift of intelligence and freedom of thought. The closed mind ill serves him. Faith has been likened to a pair of legs – like them it grows strong through exercise. The faith he requires, and which we must seek, is faith well tested in the world and not laid to rest in isolation from it.

Untested faith is rarely lost since it is never free. I believe God would rather we took the risk with him, and he with us.

Where Faith Falls short

I have faith . . . help me where faith falls short.

MARK 9.24 NEB

For our life is a matter of faith, not of sight.

2 CORINTHIANS 5.7 GNB

To have faith is to be sure of the things we hope for, to be certain of the things we cannot see.

HEBREWS 11.1 GNB

Dead Faith

Faith which does not doubt is dead faith.

MIGUEL DE UNAMUNO

Holding Fast

Faith is a power, pre-eminently, of holding fast to an unseen power of goodness.

MATTHEW ARNOLD

Believers' Doubts

I have never found anyone, however religious and devout, who didn't sometimes experience withdrawal of grace, or feel a lessening of devotion.

THOMAS À KEMPIS

Good from Everything

I believe that God can and intends to let good spring from everything, even from what is most evil. For this he needs human beings who know how to turn all things to the good. I believe that God purposes to give us in every crisis as much power of resistance as we need. But he does not give it to us in advance, in order that we shall rely not on ourselves but on him alone. In such faith, all fear of the future would necessarily be overcome. I believe that even our defects and errors are not in vain, and that it is no more difficult for God to deal with them than with our supposed good deeds. I believe that God is not a timeless *fatum*, but rather that he awaits and responds to true prayer and responsible actions.

DIETRICH BONHOEFFER

I Believe

I believe in the sun even when it is not shining.
I believe in love even when I cannot feel it.
I believe in God, even when he is silent.

WRITTEN ON A WALL IN COLOGNE
BY A JEWISH PRISONER

Into the Unknown

And I said to the man who stood at the gate of
the year:
'Give me a light, that I may tread safely into the
unknown!'
And he replied:
'Go out into the darkness and put your hand
into the Hand of God.
That shall be to you better than light and safer
than a known way.'
So I went forth, and finding the Hand of God,
trod gladly into the night.
And he led me toward the hills and the breaking
of day in the lone East.

So, heart, be still!
What need our little life,
Our human life, to know,
If God hath comprehension?
In all the dizzy strife
Of things both high and low
God hideth his intention.

M. LOUISE HASKINS

By Faith Alone

Strong Son of God, immortal Love,
Whom we, that have not seen Thy face,
 By faith, and faith alone, embrace,
Believing where we cannot prove;

We have but faith: we cannot know;
 For knowledge is of things we see;
 And yet we trust it comes from Thee,
A beam in darkness: let it grow.

ALFRED TENNYSON

Encouraged by their Example

Lord God, in whom, down the ages, so many
have effectually placed their trust: apostles,
prophets, saints, and martyrs, along with that
great company whose names have no memorial;
encouraged by their example, I come to you with
confidence to ask that this day:
 though my hold on you may be insecure,
  yet you will firmly keep your hold on me;
 though I may not reach complete certainty,
  my faith in your good providence may be
   unswerving;
 though I do not look for safety in earthly
   things,
  my loyalty to you may remain unshaken.

EVERYDAY PRAYERS

134

Our Faith is Small

Lord Jesus, we feel our faith is small and our achievements for you even smaller. But you taught us that size does not matter; even something as tiny as a mustard seed grows into a large bush. May this prove true of our faith and service, so that the good work you have begun in us may one day be perfected.

PRAYERS FOR THE CHURCH COMMUNITY

Hope Dimmed

Two men went climbing in the Pyrenees. In the night the younger man was awakened by a howling wind so strong it uprooted his tent and blew him to the edge of a dangerous precipice. There he hung on by his fingernails, crying in despair: 'Oh God, this is the end of the world!'

The older man, who was struggling to help him, called back, 'No, it's not that. This is how the dawn comes up in the Pyrenees.'

There are many occasions in life that cause us to cry out like that – circumstances that suggest the end of our world, but just as often, in the midst of darkness and despair, the light of hope has dawned – just as the morning breaks in the Pyrenees.

'Where there's life, there's hope', we say, and that is true, but it is just as true that where there is hope, there is life. Lose hope and we lose incentive and motivation; we lose the will to fight and win, and we miss the achievement that could have been ours.

Research into the effects of imprisonment during the Second World War reveals that the prisoners of war who endured it best were those who lived in hope of a better future. Anticipating brighter times enabled them to look beyond the present darkness and keep their morale high.

Real hope does this, and it is a precious possession. It must be real hope, of course, and not a vague wishful longing. The strongest hope is firmly realistic: it faces the worst that might happen but anticipates the best that can happen through personal faith and effort. If we add to such hope the Gospels' account of Easter morning followed Good Friday, and open our lives to the enabling power of the Holy Spirit, no darkness will ever extinguish the light of hope in us.

The Source of Hope

The Lord is near to those who are discouraged;
he saves those who have lost all hope.

PSALM 34.18 GNB

Answer me now, Lord! I have lost all hope.

PSALM 143.7 GNB

When hope is crushed, the heart is crushed,
but a wish come true fills you with joy.

PROVERBS 13.12 GNB

May God, the source of hope, fill you with all joy and peace by means of your faith in him, so that your hope will continue to grow by the power of the Holy Spirit.

ROMANS 15.13 GNB

Living Through the Night

He who wants to enjoy the glory of the sunrise
must live through the night.

ANONYMOUS

The Land is Bright

Say not – the struggle nought availeth,
The labour and the wounds are vain,
The enemy faints not, nor faileth –
And as things have been, they remain!

For while the tired waves, vainly breaking,
Seem here no painful inch to gain,
Far back, through creeks and inlets making,
Comes silent – flooding in – the main.

And not by eastern windows only,
When daylight comes, comes in the light;
In front, the sun climbs slow – how slowly!
But westward – look! the land is bright.

ARTHUR HUGH CLOUGH

Hope Breaking Loose

Hope is the struggle of the soul, breaking loose
from what is perishable, and attesting her
eternity.

HERMAN MELVILLE

Sunset to Dawn

Christ has turned all our sunsets into dawns.

CLEMENT OF ALEXANDRIA

In Whom is All our Hope

Eternal God, in whom is all our hope in life, in death, and to all eternity: grant that, rejoicing in the eternal life which is ours in Christ, we may face whatever the future holds in store for us calm and unafraid, always confident that neither death nor life can part us from your love in Jesus Christ our Lord.

JAMES M. TODD

The Courage to Hope

My Lord God, give me once more the courage to hope; merciful God, let me hope once again, fructify my barren and infertile mind.

SØREN KIERKEGAARD

Lord of All Hopefulness

Lord God,
the scripture says you make all things new.
Make all things new this day.
Give us such hope in you
that we become optimistic about everyone and
    everything else,
Lord of all hopefulness, Lord of the future,
lead us forward with a light step and a
    courageous heart;
to your honour and glory,
and for the sake of Jesus Christ,
your Son, our Saviour.

JAMIE WALLACE

Confidence Shattered

A series of personal sorrows and a frightful accident left Stella drained of confidence; in fact, much of her life was marred by trouble, and on her own admission she was 'accident prone'.

An only child, she lost her mother at fifteen; her father remarried, but she and her step-mother never got on, resulting in a rift between Stella and her father. Her father died too, a month before she married, and she felt 'orphaned', although now she had a husband.

After four years of marriage he left her to live with another woman – of all people, her bridesmaid and best friend. It was a bitter let down. They had no children, and her loneliness was severe. She had a nervous breakdown, lost her job as a secretary, and on a road journey home from an interview for a post, her mini was hit by a van cornering too fast. She was trapped inside for an hour, and suffered bad injuries to her chest and legs.

It took Stella many months to recover from her physical injuries, but longer again to regain her confidence in people, in motoring, and in life in general. Even her faith wavered for a while under her trials.

Happily she has remarried and has a loving

husband, she holds a steady, pleasant job, and is a faithful member of her church.

Self-confidence is important to our wellbeing, and when it is shattered or dented we do not function properly. We need to believe in ourselves and our ability to meet challenges, so its recovery is vital.

Confidence in ourselves and faith in God are related. If we have faith to believe that God believes in us, that he trusts us and wants us as his co-workers, then we can make our way in the world with true confidence and pride.

Trust not Fear

But I had nearly lost confidence;
my faith was almost gone.

PSALM 73.2 GNB

God is my saviour; I will trust him and not be afraid.

ISAIAH 12.2 GNB

Let us be brave, then, and approach God's throne, where there is grace. There we will receive mercy and find grace to help us just when we need it.

HEBREWS 4.16 GNB

Healing Wounds

God says to man: 'With thy very wounds I will heal thee.'

THE TALMUD

He Will Take Care of You

Do not look forward to what might happen tomorrow; the same everlasting Father who cares for you today, will take care of you tomorrow and every day. Either he will shield you from suffering or he will give you unfailing strength to bear it. Be at peace, then, and put aside all anxious thoughts and imaginings.

ST FRANCIS DE SALES

Confident Hope

Trusting in him who can go with me, and remain with you, and be everywhere for good, let us confidently hope that all will yet be well.

ABRAHAM LINCOLN

Confidence in People

Lord, I've had so many bad things happen to me that my confidence in people is rock-bottom, and I don't really know who to trust. It's a horrid feeling, and hurts me inside, because at heart I'm honest, open and trusting. Please help me; save me from further despair so that I can be a better person to live with, and more useful in your service. Thank you for the assurance that *you* will never let me down.

DAVID M. OWEN

As Hidden Blessings

O God, we cry out to Thee in the time of our trouble. For some sickness has taken hold, for others doubts have assailed them, others again have lost employment. Help us to remember the song of hope we would always sing in our days of prosperity and peace. Have Thine own way with our lives, teach us to see our troubles as hidden blessings. You are our changeless God who loves us even when life tumbles in with all its problems and trials. Deepen our faith in that love, through Jesus Christ our Lord. Amen.

WILLIAM H. KADEL

Animate us to Cheerfulness

O God, animate us to cheerfulness. May we have a joyful sense of our blessings, learn to look on the bright circumstances of our lot, and maintain a perpetual contentedness. Preserve us from despondency and from yielding to dejection. Teach us that nothing can hurt us if, with true loyalty of affection, we keep Thy commandments and take refuge in Thee.

WILLIAM E. CHANNING

Work Deprived

Much has been said of work as the curse of Adam – a reference to Genesis 3.17 – but this is misleading and derogatory. An earlier verse, Genesis 2.15, gives work its truer connotation: God placed man in the garden of Eden 'to till and care for it' (NEB). In other words, work is part of God's original purpose contributing to human dignity and usefulness, and not divine punishment contrived as an afterthought.

If curse there is, or at least shame, it lies not in work but redundancy – the failure of men and women to find work to do; the enforced joblessness of skilled and able-bodied people who carry inside the hurt of idleness and rejection.

A man who had lost his job said to me, 'Now that I'm out of work I feel ashamed for those times when I grumbled about the work I had to do.'

Employment gives us money for our physical needs; but more: it gives us a reason for living, and is an expression of usefulness and self-respect. Why learn skills we have no intention of using? Why acquire a caring spirit unless we are to put it into practice? Work provides us daily with colleagues, friends and conversation, and we have the satisfaction of knowing that our personal effort is contributing to the welfare of our community and to the world at large. The unemployment queue is the awful frustrator and often the death-knell of such virtues and blessings.

Strange as it seems, retirement from work can also be hard to accept and adjust to when these same benefits are withdrawn, and the period of adjustment can be very difficult. It was said of one prominent politician that the harness that weighed him down also bore him up, and when the harness was removed he collapsed. His was an extreme case, I am sure, but it highlights the importance of having a satisfying job to do, and calls for our sensitivity toward those missing their work through redundancy or retirement.

Work

Then people go out to do their work and keep working until evening.

PSALM 104.23 GNB

Your work will provide for your needs.

PSALM 128.2 GNB

'Why are you wasting the whole day here doing nothing?' he asked them. 'No one hired us,' they answered.

MATTHEW 20.6–7 GNB

Being Unemployed

There are several clear stages in being unemployed. In some ways it is rather like a bereavement. First comes shock: 'Is this really happening to me?' Then comes anger: 'Why me?' Occasionally there is a brief spell of relief: 'I could do with a break', but this stops when the redundancy money runs out. At this stage, when no job is in sight, despair and apathy are usual, often leading on to depression: 'It's so much effort just going on trying.' You dread the thud of another rejection letter on your doormat. Your mood swings yet once more from hope to despair.

It takes great adaptability to see the alternatives to an ordinary 'job' and immense energy to follow them up. Many people become very passive. The stress of being unemployed can lead to physical illness. It puts an emotional strain on the whole family.

NEWSLETTER FROM A CENTRE FOR THE
UNEMPLOYED

The Saddest Sight

A man willing to work, and unable to find work, is perhaps the saddest sight that fortune's inequality exhibits under this sun.

THOMAS CARLYLE

The Man with the Paralysed Hand

Work is man's sustenance and dignity,
And was my pride
Until the palsied curse –
My deadened hand inducing
Worklessness
And slow futility.

I knew nothing of a watchful eye that day,
Of cunning lawyered scheme
To trap the Healer in my cause
As Sabbath felon fit for death.
I only recollect my ready answer to his call
To stand before him and before them all;
His dauntless, stinging query
Whether good or evil should be wrought in
    Sabbath hours,
Or life destroyed or saved,
That taut, astounded silence
As likely to erupt in rage,
And then his singled, bold attention to my need:
'Stretch out your arm.'
My arm,
My hand
At once renewed,
And I was workable and free,
But he, unfree from venomed spite
Of Scribe and Pharisee.

DAVID M. OWEN

Out of Work

Thank you, Lord, because you made me, with
my talents, such as they are, my skills – all my

capacities. You didn't mean them to lie around unused. Show me where I can use them.

Thank you, Lord, because with all your other gifts you gave me resilience, a certain toughness of spirit. Show me how to make the adjustments that I have to make.

Father, I know that whatever happens to me, however unwelcome, there is always something to be learnt from it. What do you want me to learn from this experience? Show it to me.

And make me sure of this: that neither death nor life, principalities nor powers, employment nor unemployment can separate me from your love, which is shown to me in Christ Jesus my Lord.

MORE EVERYDAY PRAYERS

Retired

Lord, your creation continues, yet, in nature
and by the hand of man.
Does this too cease when man is sixty-five?
Look on his loneliness,
his feeling of un-use,
Watching others off to earn their daily bread
and he still,
mourning his loss of opportunity
to worship through labour at the thing he knows
    best.
Find for him, Lord, a new dignity in quieter
    places.
Let him still give, not necessarily of his skill,
but of the fruit of all his years,

148

And be wanted,
   and needed,
      for a little while yet.
        Lord?

ROGER BUSH

Life and Work

Give me work till my life shall end,
And Life till my work is done.

WINIFRED HOLTBY, HER EPITAPH

Possessions Taken

A man and his wife in their sixties lost the best part of their hard earned savings when the company in which they invested went bankrupt. It was a bitter blow that left them angry and insecure for some time.

Two elderly sisters who lived together had forgotten to pay the insurance premium on their house, and realised their failure when two rooms were badly damaged by fire, and expensive furniture was destroyed. Repair and replacement bills severely drained their resources, and each blamed the other for neglect.

Thieves broke into the home of an elderly couple while they were asleep, and stole valuable silver and glassware. Frightened and upset at first, they recovered their composure and sensibly admitted, 'These were only material things; it is more important that we were not hurt.'

It is grievous to lose money and possessions, and burglary is a despicable deed that causes untold distress, but we must avoid getting these things out of proportion and over-estimating their worth. Possessions are necessary, but are less important than our health, our love-relationships, friendships, and our moral and spiritual values.

Jesus was not averse to material things as such.

He presumably made and sold furniture and implements in the carpenter's shop at Nazareth; he illustrated God's kingdom by means of man-made things – houses, ploughs, clothes; he enjoyed food and approved of the giving of money to the needy. But he warned that materialism can lead to idolatry and anxiety: '. . . Where your treasure is, there will your heart be also. . . . Do not ask anxiously, 'What are we to eat? What are we to drink? What shall we wear?' . . . Your heavenly Father knows that you need them all. Set your mind on God's kingdom . . ..' (Matthew 6.21; 31–33 NEB).

We who place too much emphasis on material things should heed our Lord's perspective and warning.

Superfluous Riches

What do superfluous riches profit in this world, when you find in them neither a succour in birth nor a defence against death? For without a covering are we born into the world, without provision we depart hence, and in the grave we have no inheritance.

ST AMBROSE

The Lord, my Treasure

Riches I heed not, nor man's empty praise,
Thou mine inheritance, now and always:
Thou and thou only, first in my heart,
High King of heaven, my treasure thou art.

ANCIENT IRISH HYMN

Generous Business

John Woolman, the 18th-century Quaker, never let the demands of his business grow beyond his *real* needs. When too many customers came, he sent them elsewhere, to more needy merchants and tailors.

THOMAS R. KELLY

Wealth and Poverty

Neither is all wealth poor nor all poverty rich. The widow who cast two mites into the treasury by doing so became rich; but had she kept them, she would have remained simply 'a poor widow'.

CHRISTINA ROSSETTI

Poor but Rich

There is a story of a man whom others called poor, and who had just enough fortune to support himself in going about the country in the simplest way, and enjoying the life and beauty of it. He was once in the company of a great millionaire who was engaged in business, working at it daily and getting richer every year; and the poor man said to the millionaire, 'I am a richer man than you are.' 'How do you make that out?' said the millionaire. 'Why,' he replied, 'I have got as much money as I want, and you haven't.'

LORD GREY OF FALLODON

From Love of Earthly Treasures

Most loving Father, who hast taught us to dread nothing save the loss of thee, preserve me from faithless fears and worldly anxieties, from corrupting passions and unhallowed love of earthly treasures; and grant that no clouds of this mortal life may hide me from the light of that love which is immortal and which thou hast manifested unto us in thy son, Jesus Christ our Lord.

WILLIAM BRIGHT

All Care in Your Hands

Most dear and tender Father, our defender and nourisher, fill us with your grace that we may cast aside our blindness and attraction to material things; and may instead put all our efforts into discovering your will and obeying your law. Let us work, like the birds and the flowers, for what gives you glory leaving all care in your hands. Amen.

HENRY VIII's *PRIMER*

From Earthly Gain

From earthly gain which is heavenly loss,
Deliver us, deliver all men, good Lord.

CHRISTINA ROSSETTI

Pets Lost

The death of a family pet can be a distressing experience and cause of real bereavement. When Ceri our family West Highland died we were truly upset, and our home had a peculiar emptiness for some time.

Humans can form precious bonds with their pets, particularly (I think) with a dog. Someone has observed that a cat is a house guest whereas a dog joins the family. Dogs can help in forming relationships: a walk with a dog can bring us into contact with strangers who would otherwise pass us by. A dog can provide companionship and protection, and in special circumstances dogs are eyes for the blind and ears for the deaf. A dog can grieve when we are away, and welcome us home with warmth and affection.

More is being shown us of the therapeutic value of pet animals. Dependent upon us, they make us relate to their needs and they are genuine in their response to us, and constantly forgiving. I find that most homes for the elderly now have dogs, cats or budgerigars living along with the residents, and these creatures have their own way of helping people to relate and relax.

Jesus illustrated his deep and sacrificial love for us with a picture of a caring shepherd for his sheep, each of which he knew by name (John

10.1–16). It must have been a common feature of the time, well understood by his listeners. Though he used the image to speak of this greater love, he also gave a glimpse of the human–animal relationship that many of us have come to appreciate, which, when broken through their death, can leave us bereft.

The Lord's Hand Made Them

Even birds and animals have much they could teach you. . . . All of them know that the Lord's hand made them. It is God who directs the lives of his creatures.

JOB 12.7, 9–10 GNB

Not one sparrow falls to the ground without your Father's consent.

MATTHEW 10.29 GNB

Animals and Friends

Animals are such agreeable friends – they ask no questions, they pass no criticisms.

GEORGE ELIOT

Of this Trusting Relationship

The Bible tells of the love-relationship God has with us, saying that if he is truly our Father, he cannot allow that relationship to be broken by death. If a common sparrow enjoys God's caring, what of those intelligent and loving pets who have shared our lives and given us pleasure?

The Bible sees the bond of love between people as a precious God-given gift which cannot be destroyed. Perhaps the same can be said about the other kind of trusting relationships we share with our pet animals.

DAVID M. OWEN

Holiness and Animals

They say that a holy person creates a space around him or her in which it is easier for other people to be good; and I think that's true. And it's true also, I think, of the relationship of holy people to the animal creation. It's a constant throughout the world's religions that when people become holy, the animals and the birds and the fishes feel at home in their presence.

DAVID NICOLLS

Animals Unmeasured

For the animal shall not be measured by man. In a world older and more complete than ours they move finished and complete, gifted with extensions of the senses we have lost or never attained. They are not brethren; they are not underlings; they are other nations, caught with ourselves in the net of life and time, fellow prisoners of the splendour and travail of the earth.

HENRY BESTON

Now He's Gone

I've always loved my cat so much and now, Lord, he's dead. Perhaps you'd like me to be a bit more interested in other things or people, but his company has meant so much in my lonely life. He really seemed to care when others forgot or could not be bothered. Now he's gone, and I am so very much alone. Thank you for making animals, Lord, and for allowing us to have them. Can you teach me to love more through them?

MICHAEL HOLLINGS & ETTA GULLICK

Help us to be Very Kind

Lord Jesus Christ, who has taught us that without our Father in heaven no sparrow falls to the ground, help us to be very kind to all animals, and to our pets. May we remember that you will one day ask us if we have been good to them. Bless us as we take care of them; for your mercy's sake.

GILES AND MELVILLE HARCOURT

Grant that a Little Dog

O God, my Master, should I gain the grace
To see Thee face to face when life is ended,
Grant that a little dog, who once pretended
That I was God, may see me face to face!

B.C. BOULTER

SOURCES AND ACKNOWLEDGEMENTS

DEATH MOST COMMON

Death Knocks: Max Beerbohm (1872–1956), *Zuleika Dobson*, ch. 13.

Those Before and After Me: Dag Hammarskjöld (1905–61), *Markings* (Faber and Faber 1964), p. 163.

Involved in Mankind: John Donne (1571–1631), *Devotions upon Emergent Occasions*, Meditation XVII.

Death in Life: *The Book of Common Prayer* (1662), from 'The Burial of the Dead'.

Death Does Matter: C.S. Lewis (1898–1963), *A Grief Observed* (Faber and Faber 1961), p. 15.

Treated All Alike: Mark Twain (1835–1910) – his last words.

But Life is Immortal: Christmas Humphreys (an English Buddhist), in *The Great Mystery of Life Hereafter* (Hodder 1957), p. 91.

O Lord, Be With Us: *New Every Morning* (BBC 1973), p. 123; reproduced with permission.

Lord Have Mercy: David Adam, *Tides and Seasons* (Triangle/SPCK 1989), p. 71.

Simply For Love of You: Thomas More (1478–1535).

To Live at Ease: Virginia Sloyan, in *Death* (Liturgy Training Publications 1990).

FACING OUR FEARS

As Fear in the Dark: Francis Bacon (1561–1626), 'Of Death', in *Essays* (1625).

To Know not What or Where: John Dryden (1631–1700), *Aurengzebe* (1676).

No Tomorrow: Eric Hoffer, *The Passionate State of Mind* (1954).

Eternally Forgotten: Paul Tillich (1886–1965), *The Eternal Now* (1963).

As the Close of Hope: William Hazlitt (1778–1830), 'On the Love of Life', *The Round Table* (1817).

I Shall Love Death as Well: Rabindranath Tagore (1861–1941).

Jesus in the Garden: Leslie D. Weatherhead (1893–1976), *Psychology and Life* (Hodder 1934), p. 219.

To Live and Die: Thomas Ken (1637–1711), verse 3 of hymn 'Glory to thee, my God, this night'.

Death – my Fears: Graham Smith, article in the *Church Times*, 18 April 1980.

Fear Knocked: Wartime inscription, 'lettered at the time of Dunkirk'.

Death Be Not Proud: John Donne (1572–1631).

I Fear No Ill: Henry W. Baker (1821–77), from the hymn 'The King of love my shepherd is', based on Psalm 23.

Lord, I'm afraid: Michael Hollings and Etta Gullick, *The Shade of his Hand* (Mayhew McCrimmon 1973), p. 191.

From Griefs and Fears: Joseph Addison (1672–1719), verses 2–4 of hymn 'How are thy servants blest, O Lord!'.

Into thy Hands: Alan Paton (1903–1989), *Instrument of thy Peace*, (Fontana 1969), p. 57.

LIVING FOR DYING

Direction of Life: Joseph Addison (1672–1719), from *The Spectator*.

Dignity of thy Nature: Sir Thomas Browne (1605–82).

If a Man would Live Well: John Bunyan (1628–88), *The Pilgrim's Progress*.

Take Care: George Whitfield (1714–70).

Taught to Live and Die: Henry Suso (c. 1295–1366).

No Total Death: Elisabeth Kübler-Ross, *Death, the Final Stage of Growth*, p. 166.

Life – A Dying: Norman Pittinger, in *The British Weekly*, 29 November 1974.

As we Live, So we Die: Mother Teresa, in Desmond Doig, *Mother Teresa* (Collins 1976), p. 161.

So Be my Passing: William Ernest Henley (1849–1903).

Part of a Larger Pattern: Malcolm Muggeridge, *Jesus Rediscovered* (Collins/Fontana 1969), p. 178.

Tuning Here: John Donne, 'Hymn to God my God in my sickness'.

For Life and Death are One: Kahlil Gibran (1883–1931), *The Prophet* (Heinemann 1926).

The Lesson from Nature: John Cole, article 'The meaning of death' in *The Times*, 15 February 1986.

Death a Fulfilment: Dag Hammarskjöld, *Markings*, p. 136.

To Live Every Day: Thomas à Kempis (1380–1471).

Thanks for Life: Elizabeth, Countess of Craven (1750–1828).

And Our Work is Done: John Henry Newman (1801–90); his arrangement of a prayer by Lancelot Andrewes (1555–1626).

UNTIMELY, UNFULFILLED

Alive in Jesus: David M. Owen in *Woman's Weekly*, 28 March 1987.

The Bonding: Elizabeth Boot, in *Facing Bereavement* (Highland Books 1988), p. 57. (Her nineteen-year-old son was killed in a skiing accident.)

Further Stages of Growth: Richard Harries, *Being a Christian* (Mowbray 1981), p. 52.

Fulfilment Waits: Jack Winslow (1882–1974), *The Gate of Life* (Hodder 1970), p. 34.

The Unfinisheds: Victor Frankl, *Man's Search for Meaning* (Hodder 1964).

For One Born Dead: Elizabeth Jennings (b. 1926), *Collected Poems* (Macmillan 1967), reproduced with permission.

What Greater Pain? Euripides, *The Suppliant Women* (*c.* 421 BC).

Without Having Lived: Erich Fromm, *Man for Himself* (1947).

Sorrowing Hearts: The Guild of Health, a prayer for sorrowing parents.

Lord, I am Dying Now: Michael Hollings and Etta Gullick, *The Shade of his Hand*, p. 190.

Be Near me, Lord: verse 4 of hymn 'O sacred head sore wounded', translated by James W. Alexander.

THE TRAGIC CHOICE

Expression of Distress: Suicide Prevention Centre, *Manual for handling Telephone Calls.*

Up Against It: H.G. Wells (1866–1946) in his autobiography.

To Look at Your Life Again: Marjorie Pizer, *To You the Living* (Second Back Row Press, PO Box 43, Leura, NSW 2781, Australia).

But She Could Not Pull Out of It: Michael Hollings and Etta Gullick, *The Shade of his Hand*, p. 215.

You Alone Know What he Suffered: ibid.

Come unto Me: Simon H. Baynes, 'Meditation and Prayer for those tempted to commit suicide', based on Matthew 11.28, in *Prayers for Today's Church* (Falcon Books 1972), p. 316.

Christ my Helper: *Prayer Fellowship Handbook 1972* (United Reformed Church), p. 38.

WHEN DISASTER STRIKES

What Sort of World? C.R. North, in *The Expository Times* (June 1967), p. 278.

No Intervention: J.B. Phillips, *God Our Contemporary* (Hodder, 1960), p. 126.

To God We Cried: Henry Francis Lyte (1793–1847), from the hymn 'Whom should we love like thee?', based on Psalm 18.

God in the Midst: David C.H. Read, sermon in *The Expository Times* (March 1965), p. 193–4.

Why, Lord? *Prayer Fellowship Handbook 1978* (United Reformed Church), Day 23.

Suffering Disturbs Me: Michel Quoist, *Prayers of Life* (Gill and Son 1963), p. 66.

For Those in Trouble: Margaret Girdlestone, *Prayers for Today's Church* 277 (Falcon 1972).

Where the World Ended: Miroslav Holub (b. 1923), 'Five minutes after the air raid', translated by Ian Milner and George Theiner.

They Died For Us: Michael Davis, 'Thoughts on Remembrance Sunday', No. 597 in *Words For Worship*, compiled and edited by Christopher Campling and Michael Davis.

We Will Remember Them: Laurence Binyon (1869–1943) from *Poems For the Fallen*.

Yet We Are Friends: R.D. Brackenridge, sermon in *The Expository Times* (October 1967), pp. 25–6.

For Those Who Have Fallen: Anonymous, quoted in *Love is my Meaning* (DLT, 1973), p. 157.

For All Who Suffer: Frank Colquhoun, *Contemporary Parish Prayers* (Hodder 1976) no. 310 (adapted).

Strengthen Them, O Lord: Frederick B. Macnutt (1873–1949), *The Prayer Manual* (Mowbray 1986).

For Those of Ill-Will: In Ravensbruch concentration camp an unknown soldier is said to have written this prayer on a torn scrap of paper, and left it beside the body of a dead child.

Give Peace: *The Book of Common Prayer* (1662), Evening Prayer.

COMFORT IN SORROW

Introduction: Murray Parkes, *Bereavement* (Tavistock Publications 1972), pp. 19–20.

Enough Sorrow and Suffering: Henry W. Longfellow (1807–1882).

Wounds of the Spirit: John Henry Newman (1801–1890).

Longing: Alfred, Lord Tennyson, *In Memoriam* (1850).

Added to Suffering: Anne Morrow Lindbergh, in Ann Warren (ed.), *Facing Bereavement* (Highland Books 1988), p. 57.

Marooned in Misery: Mary Craig, *Blessings* (Hodder 1979), p. 135.

Deep Sobbing: Norah Leney, *In a Lifetime* (JMR Publishing Co., New York 1975).

Love in your Sorrow: H.C.G. Moule (1841–1920), Bishop of Durham.

We who are Left: Wilfred Gibson, *Collected Poems 1905–1925* (Macmillan 1926).

No Funeral Gloom: Ellen Terry (1848–1928), as she prepared her will.

I Would Like to Come: D.H. Lawrence, 'Call into Death', from *The Complete Poems* (Heinemann).

I'm a Widow: Paddy Yorkstone, in Shelagh Brown (ed.), *My Word* (BRF 1989), p. 44.

The Sun will Shine Again: Wendy Green, in Ann Warren (ed.), *Facing Bereavement* (Highland Books 1988), p. 89.

Jesus, Man of Tears: C.S. Song, *The Tears of Lady Meng* (Taiwan 1981) © World Council of Churches, Geneva.

All is Well: Henry Scott Holland (1847–1918), verses 4–5 of the hymn 'Grant us thy light' (altered).

Comfort Us who Mourn: *A Book of Services and Prayers* (The United Reformed Church), p. 81.

God of All Consolation: 'Pastoral Care for the Sick', in *Death* (Liturgical Training Publications, USA, 1990), p. 99.

JESUS LIVES, AND WE LIVE

Death in Vain: Charles Wesley (1707–88), from the hymn 'Christ the Lord is risen today'.

Jesus Lives: David Adam, *Tides and Seasons* (Triangle/SPCK 1989), p. 108.

On Such a Lovely Morning: Misuno Genzo, (1937–84), a Japanese poet, paraplegic, who communicated with a code based on movement of his eyelids. The poem (trans. Marjorie Tunbridge), was printed in *The Japan Christian Quarterly* (Summer 1984).

Belief in the Resurrection: J.S. Whale, *Christian Doctrine* (Collins/Fontana 1941), p. 69.

Easter Faith: William Barclay, in *The British Weekly* (February 1964).

Written Promise: Martin Luther (1483–1546).

So We May Trust Thy Love: George Appleton, *In His Name* (Edinburgh House Press, Macmillan and Co.), no. 76.

Lord, Come Alive: Rex Chapman, in *Hodder Prayers* (Hodder 1986), no. 721.

OUR HOPE OF LIFE IN HEAVEN

Hope Alive: Johann Wolfgang von Goethe (1749–1832).

Eternal Spring: Victor Hugo (1802–85).

The Sea Has Another Shore: H.E. Fosdick (1878–1969).

As the Seed: George Macdonald (1824–1905).

Into Eternity: Joan Brockelsby, *A Fold in My Thinking* (Beldon Books).

Heaven is God: Elisabeth of the Trinity (d. 1908), a French Carmelite nun who died at an early age.

Carry Me Home: Afro-American Spiritual.

Where I Live By Sight: John Bunyan (1628–88).

As Strangers Here: Isaac Watts, verse 4 of the hymn 'Blest be the everlasting God'.

He Shall Suffice Me: Frederick William Henry Myers (1843–1901), verse 4 of the hymn 'Hark what a sound'.

Heavenly Vision: John Donne (1571–1631).

Shall I One Day See Thee: John Henry Newman (1801–90).

Begin Heaven On Earth: Christina Rossetti (1831–94).

In Heaven to See Thy Face: William Bullock (1798–1874) and Henry Williams Baker (1821–77), verse 5 of the hymn 'We love the place, O God'.

REUNITED IN LOVE

For Ever and Always: Alexander Schmorell, in a letter to his parents before his execution by the Nazis in May 1943.

As Face to Face: Robert Louis Stevenson (1850–1894).

To Die for Each Other: Coventry Patmore (1823–96.

Unbreakable Love: George Appleton (b. 1902) in *The Daily Telegraph*.

With Our Loved Ones: Elizabeth Barrett Browning (1806–61), *Sonnets from the Portuguese*.

Together Always: Kahlil Gibran (1883–1931), *The Prophet*.

Inspired by Their Example: *A Book of Services and Prayers* (URC 1980), pp. 78–9.

Lift Our Eyes to That Day: Ian D. Bunting, in *Prayers For Today's Church* (Falcon 1972), no. 112.

THE GREAT COMMUNION

One Family, One Church: Charles Wesley, verses 2 and 3 of 'Come, let us join our friends above'.

Joined in Prayer: Richard Harries, *Being a Christian* (Mowbray 1981), pp. 60–2.

A Crossing the World: William Penn (1644–1718).

One in Christ: Sergius Bulgakov (1903–47).

Remember our Brothers and Sisters: Adapted from a Roman Catholic Requiem in *Contemporary Parish Prayers*, no. 242.

United to Thyself: William Temple (1881–1944).

The Unseen Cloud of Witnesses: William Hampson.

HEALTH DIMINISHED

Introduction: The quotation is from Isaak Walton (1593–1683), *The Compleat Angler*, 'Epistle to the Reader'.

I Wrote It: William Barclay, *Letters to the Seven Churches* (SCM 1957), p. 22.

Painful Prayers: John Bunyan (1628–88).

Learning Through Suffering: George Eliot (1819–80).

Scars to Show: Elbert Hubbard (1856–1915).

A Gift: D.M. Prescott (compiler), *A New Day*, p. 281.

Life Worth Living: *A Brave Heart* (Century Hutchinson Ltd 1989), pp. 58–9. Joanne Gillespie's diary described her fight against a recurring brain tumour.

Suffering With Us: James Casson, 'Dying, the Greatest Adventure', in Ann Warren (ed.), *Facing Bereavement* (Highland Books 1988), p. 168.

At the Foot of the Cross: William Temple, *Palm Sunday to Easter* (SCM 1942), p. 32.

Filled With His Presence: Paul Claudel (d. 1955).

Refuge and Repose: J.H. Oldham, *A New Day* (Blandford Press 1957), p. 16.

The Pain is Still there: Max Pauli.

For All in Pain: George Appleton, *Daily Prayer and Praise* (United Society for Christian Literature, Lutterworth Press 1962), no. 63.

Comfort and Succour: *The Book of Common Prayer* (1662), from the Order for Holy Communion.

At Evening: St Augustine of Hippo (354–430).

AGE WEARIED

Turn to Gold: G.K. Chesterton (1874–1936), *Collected Poems* (Methuen 1938).

Inwardly Stronger: William Blake (1757–1827).

Enriching the Years: Helen R. Lee, *The Growing Years* (Falcon Books 1963), pp. 72–3.

Old and Lovely: Wynford G. Whittaker

Love and Hope: Father George Congreve, SSJE.

Being Old: Carolyn Hooper

Beautiful Old Age: D.H. Lawrence, *Complete poems.*

More Patient and Loving: Hollings and Gullick, *The Shade of His Hand*, p. 143.

Not Easy to Accept: Monica Furlong, in *Short Prayers for the Long Day* (Collins 1978), p. 135.

FACULTIES IMPAIRED

A Kept Memory: Sara Teasdale, 'The Coin', in *Flame and Shadow* (1920).

Forgetting: Thomas Fuller (1608–61), *Gnomologia.*

Yet Will I Remember Thee: William Cowper (1731–1800), verse 3 of the hymn 'Hark, my soul'.

Hardships of Blindness: From a newsletter for the London Association for the Blind (1991).

How My Light is Spent: John Milton (1608–1674), 'On his blindness'.

'Hearing' Music: Evelyn Glennie, *Good Vibrations* (Hutchinson 1990), pp. 89, 170.

Losing Sight: William Barclay, *Prayers for Help and Healing* (Collins 1968).

Going Deaf: Hollings and Gullick, *The Shade of His Hand*, p. 103.

RELATIONSHIPS BROKEN

Indescribably Hurt: Anonymous, 1991.

Marriage Build-Up: Joseph Fort Newton, in *Prayer Fellowship Handbook 1988* (URC), February 14.

Me, a Neighbour: Werner and Lotte Pelz.

Love's Desire: M.C. D'Arcy (1888–1976).

Your Loneliness: Dag Hammarskjöld, *Markings* (Faber 1964), p. 85.

God as Friend: Thomas Fuller (1608–61).

I Am My Parents: Michel Quoist, *Meet Christ and Live* (Macmillan 1973), p. 137.

Family Estrangement: Martin Parsons, in *New Parish Prayers*, no. 496.

Stand With Us: *More Everyday Prayers* (National Christian Education Council 1982), p. 21.

FAITH WEAKENED

Dead Faith: Miguel de Unamuno (1864–1936), Spanish philosopher, poet, novelist.

Holding Fast: Matthew Arnold (1822–88).

Believers' Doubts: Thomas à Kempis (1380–1471)

Good from Everything: Dietrich Bonhoeffer, *Dying We Live* (Fontana 1956), p. 192.

Into the Unknown: M. Louise Haskins (1875–1957).

By Faith Alone: Alfred, Lord Tennyson, verses 1 and 5 of hymn.

Encouraged by Their Example: *Everyday Prayers* (NCEC), p. 67.

Our Faith is Small: *Prayers for the Church Community* (NCEC), no. 69.

HOPE DIMMED

The Land is Bright: Arthur Hugh Clough (1819–61).

Hope Breaking Loose: Herman Melville (1819–91).

Sunset to Dawn: Clement of Alexandria (*c.* 150–215), theologian.

In Whom is All our Hope: James M. Todd in Frank Colquhoun (ed.), *Contemporary Parish Prayers* (Hodder 1975), no. 130.

The Courage to Hope: Søren Kierkegaard (1813–55), Danish theologian.

Lord of All Hopefulness: Jamie Wallace (b. 1928) in *Hodder Prayers*, no. 512.

CONFIDENCE SHATTERED

He Will Take Care of You: St Francis de Sales (1567–1622).

Confident Hope: Abraham Lincoln (1809–65).

As Hidden Blessings: William Kadel (adapted).

Animate Us to Cheerfulness: William E. Channing (1780–1842).

WORK DEPRIVED

The Saddest Sight: Thomas Carlyle (1795–1881).
The Man With the Paralysed Hand: David M. Owen, based on Matthew 12.9–14, Mark 3.1–6, Luke 6.6–11.
Out of Work: *More Everyday Prayers* (NCEC 1982), p. 75.
Retired: Roger Bush, *Prayers for Pagans*.
Life and Work: Winifred Holtby (1886–1931), her epitaph.

POSSESSIONS TAKEN

Superfluous Riches: St Ambrose (*c.* 329–397), *Epistles*.
The Lord, My Treasure: Verse 4 of ancient Irish hymn 'Be thou my vision', trans. by Mary E. Byrne and Eleanor H. Hull.
Generous Business: Thomas R. Kelly (1769–1854).
Wealth and Poverty: Christina Rossetti (1830–94).
Poor but Rich: Lord Gray of Falloden (1862–1933).
From Love of Earthly Treasures: William Bright (1824–1901).
All Care in Your Hands: Henry VIII's *Primer* (1543).

PETS LOST

Animals and Friends: George Eliot (1819–80).
Of This Trusting Relationship: David M. Owen, *Woman's Weekly*, 22 June 1985.
Holiness and Animals: David Nicolls, quoted in *The Case Against God* (Collins 1984), p. 61.
Animals Unmeasured: Henry Beston, *The Outermost House*.
Now He's Gone: Hollings and Gullick, *The Shade of His Hand*, p. 216.
Help Us to be Very Kind: Giles and Melville Harcourt, *Short Prayers for the Long Day*, p. 22.
Grant that a Little Dog: B.C. Boulter, *Hodder Prayers*, no. 830.